Contents

BANANA CRUMB MUFFINS

Servings: 10 | Prep: 15m | Cooks: 20m | Total: 35m

NUTRITION FACTS

Calories: 263 | Carbohydrates: 46g | Fat: 8.1g | Protein: 3.2g | Cholesterol: 38mg

INGREDIENTS

- 1 1/2 cups all-purpose flour
- 1 egg, lightly beaten
- 1 teaspoon baking soda
- 1/3 cup butter, melted
- 1 teaspoon baking powder
- 1/3 cup packed brown sugar
- 1/2 teaspoon salt
- 2 tablespoons all-purpose flour
- 3 bananas, mashed
- 1/8 teaspoon ground cinnamon
- 3/4 cup white sugar
- 1 tablespoon butter

DIRECTIONS

1. Preheat oven to 375 degrees F (190 degrees C). Lightly grease 10 muffin cups, or line with muffin papers.
2. In a large bowl, mix together 1 1/2 cups flour, baking soda, baking powder and salt. In another bowl, beat together bananas, sugar, egg and melted butter. Stir the banana mixture into the flour mixture just until moistened. Spoon batter into prepared muffin cups.
3. In a small bowl, mix together brown sugar, 2 tablespoons flour and cinnamon. Cut in 1 tablespoon butter until mixture resembles coarse cornmeal. Sprinkle topping over muffins.
4. Bake in preheated oven for 18 to 20 minutes, until a toothpick inserted into center of a muffin comes out clean.

TO DIE FOR BLUEBERRY MUFFINS

Servings: 8 | Prep: 15m | Cooks: 25m | Total: 40m

NUTRITION FACTS

Calories: 383 | Carbohydrates: 56.9g | Fat: 16.1g | Protein: 4.3g | Cholesterol: 39mg

INGREDIENTS

- 1 1/2 cups all-purpose flour
- 1/3 cup milk, or more as needed
- 3/4 cup white sugar
- 1 cup fresh blueberries
- 1/2 teaspoon salt
- 1/2 cup white sugar
- 2 teaspoons baking powder
- 1/3 cup all-purpose flour
- 1/3 cup vegetable oil
- 1/4 cup butter, cubed
- 1 egg
- 1 1/2 teaspoons ground cinnamon

DIRECTIONS

1. Preheat oven to 400 degrees F (200 degrees C). Grease muffin cups or line with muffin liners.
2. Combine 1 1/2 cups flour, 3/4 cup sugar, salt and baking powder. Place vegetable oil into a 1 cup measuring cup; add the egg and add enough milk to reach the 1-cup mark. Mix this with flour mixture. Fold in blueberries. Fill muffin cups right to the top, and sprinkle with crumb topping mixture.
3. To Make Crumb Topping: Mix together 1/2 cup sugar, 1/3 cup flour, 1/4 cup butter, and 1 1/2 teaspoons cinnamon. Mix with fork, and sprinkle over muffins before baking.
4. Bake for 20 to 25 minutes in the preheated oven, or until done.

MOM'S ZUCCHINI BREAD

Servings: 24 | Prep: 20m | Cooks: 1h | Total: 1h40m | Additional: 20m

NUTRITION FACTS

Calories: 255 | Carbohydrates: 32.1g | Fat: 13.1g | Protein: 3.3g | Cholesterol: 23mg

INGREDIENTS

- 3 cups all-purpose flour
- 1 cup vegetable oil
- 1 teaspoon salt
- 2 1/4 cups white sugar
- 1 teaspoon baking soda
- 3 teaspoons vanilla extract
- 1 teaspoon baking powder
- 2 cups grated zucchini

- 1 tablespoon ground cinnamon
- 1 cup chopped walnuts
- 3 eggs

DIRECTIONS

1. Grease and flour two 8 x 4 inch pans. Preheat oven to 325 degrees F (165 degrees C).
2. Sift flour, salt, baking powder, soda, and cinnamon together in a bowl.
3. Beat eggs, oil, vanilla, and sugar together in a large bowl. Add sifted ingredients to the creamed mixture, and beat well. Stir in zucchini and nuts until well combined. Pour batter into prepared pans.
4. Bake for 40 to 60 minutes, or until tester inserted in the center comes out clean. Cool in pan on rack for 20 minutes. Remove bread from pan, and completely cool.

DOWNEAST MAINE PUMPKIN BREAD

Servings: 24 | Prep: 15m | Cooks: 50m | Total: 1h5m

NUTRITION FACTS

Calories: 263 | Carbohydrates: 40.6g | Fat: 10.3g | Protein: 3.1g | Cholesterol: 31mg

INGREDIENTS

- 1 (15 ounce) can pumpkin puree
- 2 teaspoons baking soda
- 4 eggs
- 1 1/2 teaspoons salt
- 1 cup vegetable oil
- 1 teaspoon ground cinnamon
- 2/3 cup water
- 1 teaspoon ground nutmeg
- 3 cups white sugar
- 1/2 teaspoon ground cloves
- 31/2 cups all-purpose flour
- 1/4 teaspoon ground ginger

DIRECTIONS

1. Preheat oven to 350 degrees F (175 degrees C). Grease and flour three 7x3 inch loaf pans.

2. In a large bowl, mix together pumpkin puree, eggs, oil, water and sugar until well blended. In a separate bowl, whisk together the flour, baking soda, salt, cinnamon, nutmeg, cloves and ginger. Stir the dry ingredients into the pumpkin mixture until just blended. Pour into the prepared pans.
3. Bake for about 50 minutes in the preheated oven. Loaves are done when toothpick inserted in center comes out clean.

JANET'S RICH BANANA BREAD
Servings: 15 | Prep: 10m | Cooks: 1h | Total: 1h10m

NUTRITION FACTS

Calories: 218 | Carbohydrates: 27.4g | Fat: 11.1g | Protein: 3.2g | Cholesterol: 44mg

INGREDIENTS

- 1/2 cup butter, melted
- 1 teaspoon baking soda
- 1 cup white sugar
- 1/2 teaspoon salt
- 2 eggs
- 1/2 cup sour cream
- 1 teaspoon vanilla extract
- 1/2 cup chopped walnuts
- 1 1/2 cups all-purpose flour
- 2 medium bananas, sliced

DIRECTIONS

1. Preheat oven to 350 degrees F (175 degrees C). Grease a 9x5 inch loaf pan.
2. In a large bowl, stir together the melted butter and sugar. Add the eggs and vanilla, mix well. Combine the flour, baking soda and salt, stir into the butter mixture until smooth. Finally, fold in the sour cream, walnuts and bananas. Spread evenly into the prepared pan.
3. Bake at 350 degrees F (175 degrees C) for 60 minutes, or until a toothpick inserted into the center of the loaf comes out clean. Cool loaf in the pan for 10 minutes before removing to a wire rack to cool completely.

CLONE OF A CINNABON
Servings: 12 | Prep: 20m | Cooks: 15m | Total: 3h | Additional: 2h25m

NUTRITION FACTS

Calories: 502 | Carbohydrates: 77.3g | Fat: 18.5g | Protein: 8.2g | Cholesterol: 64mg

INGREDIENTS

- 1 cup warm milk (110 degrees F/45 degrees C)
- 2 1/2 tablespoons ground cinnamon
- 2 eggs, room temperature
- 1/3 cup butter, softened
- 1/3 cup margarine, melted
- 1 (3 ounce) package cream cheese, softened
- 4 1/2 cups bread flour
- 1/4 cup butter, softened
- 1 teaspoon salt
- 1 1/2 cups confectioners' sugar
- 1/2 cup white sugar
- 1/2 teaspoon vanilla extract
- 2 1/2 teaspoons bread machine yeast
- 1/8 teaspoon salt
- 1 cup brown sugar, packed

DIRECTIONS

1. Place ingredients in the pan of the bread machine in the order recommended by the manufacturer. Select dough cycle; press Start.
2. After the dough has doubled in size turn it out onto a lightly floured surface, cover and let rest for 10 minutes. In a small bowl, combine brown sugar and cinnamon.
3. Roll dough into a 16x21-inch rectangle. Spread dough with 1/3 cup butter and sprinkle evenly with sugar/cinnamon mixture. Roll up dough and cut into 12 rolls. Place rolls in a lightly greased 9x13 inch baking pan. Cover and let rise until nearly doubled, about 30 minutes. Meanwhile, preheat oven to 400 degrees F (200 degrees C).
4. Bake rolls in preheated oven until golden brown, about 15 minutes. While rolls are baking, beat together cream cheese, 1/4 cup butter, confectioners' sugar, vanilla extract and salt. Spread frosting on warm rolls before serving.

CLONE OF A CINNABON

Servings: 9 | Prep: 15m | Cooks: 40m | Total: 55m

NUTRITION FACTS

Calories: 284 | Carbohydrates: 39.1g | Fat: 12.2g | Protein: 4.8g | Cholesterol: 59mg

INGREDIENTS

- 1/2 cup butter
- 1/2 teaspoon baking soda
- 2/3 cup white sugar
- 1 cup cornmeal
- 2 eggs
- 1 cup all-purpose flour
- 1 cup buttermilk
- 1/2 teaspoon salt

DIRECTIONS

1. Preheat oven to 375 degrees F (175 degrees C). Grease an 8 inch square pan.
2. Melt butter in large skillet. Remove from heat and stir in sugar. Quickly add eggs and beat until well blended. Combine buttermilk with baking soda and stir into mixture in pan. Stir in cornmeal, flour, and salt until well blended and few lumps remain. Pour batter into the prepared pan.
3. Bake in the preheated oven for 30 to 40 minutes, or until a toothpick inserted in the center comes out clean.

AMISH WHITE BREAD

Servings: 24 | Prep: 20m | Cooks: 40m | Total: 2h30m | Additional: 1h30m

NUTRITION FACTS

Calories: 168 | Carbohydrates: 30.7g | Fat: 2.9g | Protein: 4.4g | Cholesterol: 0mg

INGREDIENTS

- 2 cups warm water (110 degrees F/45 degrees C)
- 1 1/2 teaspoons salt
- 2/3 cup white sugar
- 1/4 cup vegetable oil
- 1 1/2 tablespoons active dry yeast
- 6 cups bread flour

DIRECTIONS

1. In a large bowl, dissolve the sugar in warm water, and then stir in yeast. Allow to proof until yeast resembles a creamy foam.

2. Mix salt and oil into the yeast. Mix in flour one cup at a time. Knead dough on a lightly floured surface until smooth. Place in a well oiled bowl, and turn dough to coat. Cover with a damp cloth. Allow to rise until doubled in bulk, about 1 hour.

3. Punch dough down. Knead for a few minutes, and divide in half. Shape into loaves, and place into two well oiled 9x5 inch loaf pans. Allow to rise for 30 minutes, or until dough has risen 1 inch above pans.

4. Bake at 350 degrees F (175 degrees C) for 30 minutes.

BANANA SOUR CREAM BREAD

Servings: 32 | Prep: 10m | Cooks: 1h | Total: 1h10m

NUTRITION FACTS

Calories: 263 | Carbohydrates: 40.1g | Fat: 10.4g | Protein: 3.7g | Cholesterol: 35mg

INGREDIENTS

- 1/4 cup white sugar
- 2 teaspoons vanilla extract
- 1 teaspoon ground cinnamon
- 2 teaspoons ground cinnamon
- 3/4 cup butter
- 1/2 teaspoon salt
- 3 cups white sugar
- 3 teaspoons baking soda
- 3 eggs
- 4 1/2 cups all-purpose flour
- 6 very ripe bananas, mashed
- 1 cup chopped walnuts (optional)
- 1 (16 ounce) container sour cream

DIRECTIONS

1. Preheat oven to 300 degrees F (150 degrees C). Grease four 7x3 inch loaf pans. In a small bowl, stir together 1/4 cup white sugar and 1 teaspoon cinnamon. Dust pans lightly with cinnamon and sugar mixture.

2. In a large bowl, cream butter and 3 cups sugar. Mix in eggs, mashed bananas, sour cream, vanilla and cinnamon. Mix in salt, baking soda and flour. Stir in nuts. Divide into prepared pans.

3. Bake for 1 hour, until a toothpick inserted in center comes out clean.

BANANA MUFFINS

Servings: 12 | Prep: 10m | Cooks: 25m | Total: 35m

NUTRITION FACTS

Calories: 187 | Carbohydrates: 32.3g | Fat: 5.8g | Protein: 2.6g | Cholesterol: 29mg

INGREDIENTS

- 1 1/2 cups all-purpose flour
- 3 large bananas, mashed
- 1 teaspoon baking powder
- 3/4 cup white sugar
- 1 teaspoon baking soda
- 1 egg
- 1/2 teaspoon salt
- 1/3 cup butter, melted

DIRECTIONS

1. Preheat oven to 350 degrees F (175 degrees C). Coat muffin pans with non-stick spray, or use paper liners. Sift together the flour, baking powder, baking soda, and salt; set aside.

J.P.'S BIG DADDY BISCUITS

Servings: 6 | Prep: 30m | Cooks: 15m | Total: 45m

NUTRITION FACTS

Calories: 282 | Carbohydrates: 36.4g | Fat: 12.6g | Protein: 5.6g | Cholesterol: 3mg

INGREDIENTS

- 2 cups all-purpose flour
- 1 tablespoon white sugar
- 1 tablespoon baking powder
- 1/3 cup shortening
- 1 teaspoon salt
- 1 cup milk

DIRECTIONS

1. Preheat oven to 425 degrees F (220 degrees C).
2. In a large bowl, whisk together the flour, baking powder, salt, and sugar. Cut in the shortening until the mixture resembles coarse meal. Gradually stir in milk until dough pulls away from the side of the bowl.
3. Turn out onto a floured surface, and knead 15 to 20 times. Pat or roll dough out to 1 inch thick. Cut biscuits with a large cutter or juice glass dipped in flour. Repeat until all dough is used. Brush off the excess flour, and place biscuits onto an ungreased baking sheet.
4. Bake for 13 to 15 minutes in the preheated oven, or until edges begin to brown.

GOLDEN SWEET CORNBREAD

Servings: 12 | Prep: 10m | Cooks: 25m | Total: 35m

NUTRITION FACTS

Calories: 189 | Carbohydrates: 28.2g | Fat: 7.4g | Protein: 3.1g | Cholesterol: 17mg

INGREDIENTS

- 1 cup all-purpose flour
- 3 1/2 teaspoons baking powder
- 1 cup yellow cornmeal
- 1 egg
- 2/3 cup white sugar
- 1 cup milk
- 1 teaspoon salt
- 1/3 cup vegetable oil

DIRECTIONS

1. Preheat oven to 400 degrees F (200 degrees C). Spray or lightly grease a 9 inch round cake pan.
2. In a large bowl, combine flour, cornmeal, sugar, salt and baking powder. Stir in egg, milk and vegetable oil until well combined. Pour batter into prepared pan.
3. Bake in preheated oven for 20 to 25 minutes, or until a toothpick inserted into the center of the loaf comes out clean.

BEST BREAD MACHINE BREAD

Servings: 12 | Prep: 10m | Cooks: 40m | Total: 3h | Additional: 2h10m

NUTRITION FACTS

Calories: 174 | Carbohydrates: 27.1g | Fat: g | Protein: 4.3g | Cholesterol: 0mg

INGREDIENTS

- 1 cup warm water (110 degrees F/45 degrees C)
- 1/4 cup vegetable oil
- 2 tablespoons white sugar
- 3 cups bread flour
- 1 (.25 ounce) package bread machine yeast
- 1 teaspoon salt

DIRECTIONS

1. Place the water, sugar and yeast in the pan of the bread machine. Let the yeast dissolve and foam for 10 minutes. Add the oil, flour and salt to the yeast. Select Basic or White Bread setting, and press Start.

SWEET DINNER ROLLS

Servings: 16 | Prep: 20m | Cooks: 20m | Total: 2h20m | Additional: 1h40m

NUTRITION FACTS

Calories: 192 | Carbohydrates: 27.1g | Fat: 7.5g | Protein: 3.9g | Cholesterol: 30mg

INGREDIENTS

- 1/2 cup warm water (110 degrees F/45 degrees C)
- 1 teaspoon salt
- 1/2 cup warm milk
- 3 3/4 cups all-purpose flour
- 1 egg
- 1 (.25 ounce) package active dry yeast
- 1/3 cup butter, softened
- 1/4 cup butter, softened
- 1/3 cup white sugar

DIRECTIONS

1. Place water, milk, egg, 1/3 cup butter, sugar, salt, flour and yeast in the pan of the bread machine in the order recommended by the manufacturer. Select Dough/Knead and First Rise Cycle; press Start.
2. When cycle finishes, turn dough out onto a lightly floured surface. Divide dough in half. Roll each half into a 12 inch circle, spread 1/4 cup softened butter over entire round. Cut each circle into 8 wedges. Roll wedges starting at wide end; roll gently but tightly. Place point side down on ungreased cookie sheet. Cover with clean kitchen towel and put in a warm place, let rise 1 hour. Meanwhile, preheat oven to 400 degrees F (200 degrees C).
3. Bake in preheated oven for 10 to 15 minutes, until golden.

BLUEBERRY ZUCCHINI BREAD

Servings: 12 | Prep: 15m | Cooks: 50m | Total: 1h45m | Additional: 40m

NUTRITION FACTS

Calories: 461 | Carbohydrates: 66.8g | Fat: 19.9g | Protein: 5.3g | Cholesterol: 47mg

INGREDIENTS

- 3 eggs, lightly beaten
- 1 teaspoon salt
- 1 cup vegetable oil
- 1 teaspoon baking powder
- 3 teaspoons vanilla extract
- 1/4 teaspoon baking soda
- 2 1/4 cups white sugar
- 1 tablespoon ground cinnamon
- 2 cups shredded zucchini
- 1 pint fresh blueberries
- 3 cups all-purpose flour

DIRECTIONS

1. Preheat oven to 350 degrees F (175 degrees C). Lightly grease 4 mini-loaf pans.
2. In a large bowl, beat together the eggs, oil, vanilla, and sugar. Fold in the zucchini. Beat in the flour, salt, baking powder, baking soda, and cinnamon. Gently fold in the blueberries. Transfer to the prepared mini-loaf pans.
3. Bake 50 minutes in the preheated oven, or until a knife inserted in the center of a loaf comes out clean. Cool 20 minutes in pans, then turn out onto wire racks to cool completely.

DONUT MUFFINS

Servings: 24 | Prep: 15m | Cooks: 15m | Total: 40m | Additional: 10m

NUTRITION FACTS

Calories: 88 | Carbohydrates: 12.8g | Fat: 3.9g | Protein: 0.8g | Cholesterol: 0mg

INGREDIENTS

- 1/2 cup white sugar
- 1 cup all-purpose flour
- 1/4 cup margarine, melted
- 1/4 cup margarine, melted
- 3/4 teaspoon ground nutmeg
- 1/2 cup white sugar
- 1/2 cup milk
- 1 teaspoon ground cinnamon
- 1 teaspoon baking powder

DIRECTIONS

1. Preheat oven to 375 degrees F (190 degrees C). Grease 24 mini-muffin cups.
2. Mix 1/2 cup sugar, 1/4 cup margarine, and nutmeg in a large bowl. Stir in the milk, then mix in the baking powder and flour until just combined. Fill the prepared mini muffin cups about half full.
3. Bake in the preheated oven until the tops are lightly golden, 15 to 20 minutes.
4. While muffins are baking, place 1/4 cup of melted margarine in a bowl. In a separate bowl, mix together 1/2 cup of sugar with the cinnamon. Remove muffins from their cups, dip each muffin in the melted margarine, and roll in the sugar-cinnamon mixture. Let cool and serve.

HOMESTEADER CORNBREAD

Servings: 15 | Prep: 15m | Cooks: 30m | Total: 50m | Additional: 5m

NUTRITION FACTS

Calories: 234 | Carbohydrates: 33.1g | Fat: 9.3g | Protein: 4.9g | Cholesterol: 28mg

INGREDIENTS

- 1 1/2 cups cornmeal
- 1 teaspoon salt
- 2 1/2 cups milk

- 2/3 cup white sugar
- 2 cups all-purpose flour
- 2 eggs
- 1 tablespoon baking powder
- 1/2 cup vegetable oil

DIRECTIONS

1. Preheat oven to 400 degrees F (200 degrees C). In a small bowl, combine cornmeal and milk; let stand for 5 minutes. Grease a 9x13 inch baking pan.
2. In a large bowl, whisk together flour, baking powder, salt and sugar. Mix in the cornmeal mixture, eggs and oil until smooth. Pour batter into prepared pan.
3. Bake in preheated oven for 30 to 35 minutes, or until a knife inserted into the center of the cornbread comes out clean.

BUTTERY SOFT PRETZELS

Servings: 12 | Prep: 2h | Cooks: 10m | Total: 2h20m | Additional: 10m

NUTRITION FACTS

Calories: 237 | Carbohydrates: 48.9g | Fat: 1.7g | Protein: 5.9g | Cholesterol: 0mg

INGREDIENTS

- 4 teaspoons active dry yeast
- 1 1/2 teaspoons salt
- 1 teaspoon white sugar
- 1 tablespoon vegetable oil
- 1 1/4 cups warm water (110 degrees F/45 degrees C)
- 1/2 cup baking soda
- 5 cups all-purpose flour
- 4 cups hot water
- 1/2 cup white sugar
- 1/4 cup kosher salt, for topping

DIRECTIONS

1. In a small bowl, dissolve yeast and 1 teaspoon sugar in 1 1/4 cup warm water. Let stand until creamy, about 10 minutes.
2. In a large bowl, mix together flour, 1/2 cup sugar, and salt. Make a well in the center; add the oil and yeast mixture. Mix and form into a dough. If the mixture is dry, add one or two more tablespoons of

water. Knead the dough until smooth, about 7 to 8 minutes. Lightly oil a large bowl, place the dough in the bowl, and turn to coat with oil. Cover with plastic wrap and let rise in a warm place until doubled in size, about 1 hour.

3. Preheat oven to 450 degrees F (230 degrees C). Grease 2 baking sheets.
4. In a large bowl, dissolve baking soda in 4 cups hot water; set aside. When risen, turn dough out onto a lightly floured surface and divide into 12 equal pieces. Roll each piece into a rope and twist into a pretzel shape. Once all of the dough is shaped, dip each pretzel into the baking soda-hot water solution and place pretzels on baking sheets. Sprinkle with kosher salt.
5. Bake in preheated oven until browned, about 8 minutes.

GRANDMA JOHNSON'S SCONES

Servings: 12 | Prep: 15m | Cooks: 15m | Total: 30m

NUTRITION FACTS

Calories: 440 | Carbohydrates: 60.4g | Fat: 20.2g | Protein: 6g | Cholesterol: 65mg

INGREDIENTS

- 1 cup sour cream
- 1/4 teaspoon cream of tartar
- 1 teaspoon baking soda
- 1 teaspoon salt
- 4 cups all-purpose flour
- 1 cup butter
- 1 cup white sugar
- 1 egg
- 2 teaspoons baking powder
- 1 cup raisins (optional)

DIRECTIONS

1. In a small bowl, blend the sour cream and baking soda, and set aside.
2. Preheat oven to 350 degrees F (175 degrees C). Lightly grease a large baking sheet.
3. In a large bowl, mix the flour, sugar, baking powder, cream of tartar, and salt. Cut in the butter. Stir the sour cream mixture and egg into the flour mixture until just moistened. Mix in the raisins.
4. Turn dough out onto a lightly floured surface, and knead briefly. Roll or pat dough into a 3/4 inch thick round. Cut into 12 wedges, and place them 2 inches apart on the prepared baking sheet.
5. Bake 12 to 15 minutes in the preheated oven, until golden brown on the bottom.

NAAN

Servings: 14 | Prep: 30m | Cooks: 7m | Total: 3h | Additional: 2h23m

NUTRITION FACTS

Calories: 52 | Carbohydrates: 4.1g | Fat: 3.7g | Protein: 0.8g | Cholesterol: 22mg

INGREDIENTS

- 1 (.25 ounce) package active dry yeast
- 2 teaspoons salt
- 1 cup warm water
- 4 1/2 cups bread flour
- 1/4 cup white sugar
- 2 teaspoons minced garlic (optional)
- 3 tablespoons milk
- 1/4 cup butter, melted
- 1 egg, beaten

DIRECTIONS

1. In a large bowl, dissolve yeast in warm water. Let stand about 10 minutes, until frothy. Stir in sugar, milk, egg, salt, and enough flour to make a soft dough. Knead for 6 to 8 minutes on a lightly floured surface, or until smooth. Place dough in a well oiled bowl, cover with a damp cloth, and set aside to rise. Let it rise 1 hour, until the dough has doubled in volume.
2. Punch down dough, and knead in garlic. Pinch off small handfuls of dough about the size of a golf ball. Roll into balls, and place on a tray. Cover with a towel, and allow to rise until doubled in size, about 30 minutes.
3. During the second rising, preheat grill to high heat.
4. At grill side, roll one ball of dough out into a thin circle. Lightly oil grill. Place dough on grill, and cook for 2 to 3 minutes, or until puffy and lightly browned. Brush uncooked side with butter, and turn over. Brush cooked side with butter, and cook until browned, another 2 to 4 minutes. Remove from grill, and continue the process until all the naan has been prepared.

EXTREME BANANA NUT BREAD 'EBNB'

Servings: 24 | Prep: 20m | Cooks: 1h10m | Total: 1h30m

NUTRITION FACTS

Calories: 232 | Carbohydrates: 29.7g | Fat: 11.9g | Protein: 3.2g | Cholesterol: 51mg

INGREDIENTS

- 2 cups all-purpose flour
- 2 cups white sugar
- 1 teaspoon salt
- 2 cups mashed overripe bananas
- 2 teaspoons baking soda
- 4 eggs, beaten
- 1 cup butter or margarine
- 1 cup chopped walnuts

DIRECTIONS

1. Preheat the oven to 350 degrees F (175 degrees C). Grease and flour two 9x5 inch loaf pans.
2. Sift the flour, salt and baking soda into a large bowl. In a separate bowl, mix together the butter or margarine and sugar until smooth. Stir in the bananas, eggs, and walnuts until well blended. Pour the wet ingredients into the dry mixture, and stir just until blended. Divide the batter evenly between the two loaf pans.
3. Bake for 60 to 70 minutes in the preheated oven, until a knife inserted into the crown of the loaf comes out clean. Let the loaves cool in the pans for at least 5 minutes, then turn out onto a cooling rack, and cool completely. Wrap in aluminum foil to keep in the moisture. Ideally, refrigerate the loaves for 2 hours or more before serving.

SIMPLE WHOLE WHEAT BREAD

Servings: 36 | Prep: 20m | Cooks: 30m | Total: 3h | Additional: 2h10m

NUTRITION FACTS

Calories: 143 | Carbohydrates: 27.6g | Fat: 2.2g | Protein: 4.1g | Cholesterol: 4mg

INGREDIENTS

- 3 cups warm water (110 degrees F/45 degrees C)
- 1/3 cup honey
- 2 (.25 ounce) packages active dry yeast
- 1 tablespoon salt
- 1/3 cup honey
- 3 1/2 cups whole wheat flour
- 5 cups bread flour
- 2 tablespoons butter, melted

- 3 tablespoons butter, melted

DIRECTIONS

1. In a large bowl, mix warm water, yeast, and 1/3 cup honey. Add 5 cups white bread flour, and stir to combine. Let set for 30 minutes, or until big and bubbly.
2. Mix in 3 tablespoons melted butter, 1/3 cup honey, and salt. Stir in 2 cups whole wheat flour. Flour a flat surface and knead with whole wheat flour until not real sticky - just pulling away from the counter, but still sticky to touch. This may take an additional 2 to 4 cups of whole wheat flour. Place in a greased bowl, turning once to coat the surface of the dough. Cover with a dishtowel. Let rise in a warm place until doubled.
3. Punch down, and divide into 3 loaves. Place in greased 9 x 5 inch loaf pans, and allow to rise until dough has topped the pans by one inch.
4. Bake at 350 degrees F (175 degrees C) for 25 to 30 minutes; do not overbake. Lightly brush the tops of loaves with 2 tablespoons melted butter or margarine when done to prevent crust from getting hard. Cool completely

NINETY MINUTE CINNAMON ROLLS

Servings: 12 | Prep: 20m | Cooks: 20m | Total: 1h30m | Additional: 50m

NUTRITION FACTS

Calories: 347 | Carbohydrates: 54.9g | Fat: 12.5g | Protein: 5.1g | Cholesterol: 17mg

INGREDIENTS

- 3/4 cup milk
- 1/4 cup water
- 1/4 cup margarine, softened
- 1 egg
- 3 1/4 cups all-purpose flour
- 1 cup brown sugar, packed
- 1 (.25 ounce) package instant yeast
- 1 tablespoon ground cinnamon
- 1/4 cup white sugar
- 1/2 cup margarine, softened
- 1/2 teaspoon salt
- 1/2 cup raisins (optional)

DIRECTIONS

1. Heat the milk in a small saucepan until it bubbles, then remove from heat. Mix in margarine; stir until melted. Let cool until lukewarm.
2. In a large mixing bowl, combine 2 1/4 cup flour, yeast, white sugar and salt; mix well. Add water, egg and the milk mixture; beat well. Add the remaining flour, 1/2 cup at a time, stirring well after each addition. When the dough has just pulled together, turn it out onto a lightly floured surface and knead until smooth, about 5 minutes.
3. Cover the dough with a damp cloth and let rest for 10 minutes. Meanwhile, in a small bowl, mix together brown sugar, cinnamon, softened margarine.
4. Roll out dough into a 12x9 inch rectangle. Spread dough with margarine/sugar mixture. Sprinkle with raisins if desired. Roll up dough and pinch seam to seal. Cut into 12 equal size rolls and place cut side up in 12 lightly greased muffin cups. Cover and let rise until doubled, about 30 minutes. Preheat oven to 375 degrees F (190 degrees C).
5. Bake in the preheated oven for 20 minutes, or until browned. Remove from muffin cups to cool. Serve warm

MONKEY BREAD

Servings: 15 | Prep: 15m | Cooks: 35m | Total: 1h | Additional: 10m

NUTRITION FACTS

Calories: 418 | Carbohydrates: 61.5g | Fat: 17.7g | Protein: 5.3g | Cholesterol: 1mg

INGREDIENTS

- 3 (12 ounce) packages refrigerated biscuit dough
- 1 cup packed brown sugar
- 1 cup white sugar
- 1/2 cup chopped walnuts (optional)
- 2 teaspoons ground cinnamon
- 1/2 cup raisins
- 1/2 cup margarine

DIRECTIONS

1. Preheat oven to 350 degrees F (175 degrees C). Grease one 9 or 10 inch tube/Bundt® pan.
2. Mix white sugar and cinnamon in a plastic bag. Cut biscuits into quarters. Shake 6 to 8 biscuit pieces in the sugar cinnamon mix. Arrange pieces in the bottom of the prepared pan. Continue until all biscuits are coated and placed in pan. If using nuts and raisins, arrange them in and among the biscuit pieces as you go along.

3. In a small saucepan, melt the margarine with the brown sugar over medium heat. Boil for 1 minute. Pour over the biscuits.
4. Bake at 350 degrees F (175 degrees C) for 35 minutes. Let bread cool in pan for 10 minutes, then turn out onto a plate. Do not cut! The bread just pulls apart.

PUMPKIN BREAD

Servings: 36 | Prep: 15m | Cooks: 1h | Total: 1h15m

NUTRITION FACTS

Calories: 247 | Carbohydrates: 36.8g | Fat: 10.3g | Protein: 3g | Cholesterol: 31mg

INGREDIENTS

- 3 cups canned pumpkin puree
- 1 1/2 teaspoons baking soda
- 1 1/2 cups vegetable oil
- 1 1/2 teaspoons salt
- 4 cups white sugar
- 1 1/2 teaspoons ground cinnamon
- 6 eggs
- 1 1/2 teaspoons ground nutmeg
- 4 3/4 cups all-purpose flour
- 1 1/2 teaspoons ground cloves
- 1 1/2 teaspoons baking powder

DIRECTIONS

1. Preheat the oven to 350 degrees F (175 degrees C). Grease and flour three 9x5 inch loaf pans.
2. In a large bowl, mix together the pumpkin, oil, sugar, and eggs. Combine the flour, baking powder, baking soda, salt, cinnamon, nutmeg, and cloves; stir into the pumpkin mixture until well blended. Divide the batter evenly between the prepared pans.
3. Bake in preheated oven for 45 minutes to 1 hour. The top of the loaf should spring back when lightly pressed.

PEAS AND GUMBO

Servings: 12 | Prep: 20m | Cooks: 20m | Total: 1h | Additional: 20m

NUTRITION FACTS

INGREDIENTS

- 2 cups all-purpose flour
- 1 1/4 teaspoons vanilla
- 1 teaspoon baking powder
- 1 1/2 cups chopped apples
- 1/2 teaspoon baking soda
- 1/3 cup packed brown sugar
- 1/2 teaspoon salt
- 1 tablespoon all-purpose flour
- 1/2 cup butter
- 1/8 teaspoon ground cinnamon
- 1 cup white sugar
- 1 tablespoon butter
- 2 eggs

DIRECTIONS

1. Preheat oven to 375 degrees F (190 degrees C). Grease a 12 cup muffin pan.
2. In a medium bowl, mix flour, baking powder, baking soda and salt.
3. In a large bowl, beat together butter, sugar and eggs until smooth. Mix in vanilla. Stir in apples, and gradually blend in the flour mixture. Spoon the mixture into the prepared muffin pan.
4. In a small bowl, mix brown sugar, flour and cinnamon. Cut in butter until mixture is like coarse crumbs. Sprinkle over tops of mixture in muffin pan.
5. Bake 20 minutes in the preheated oven, or until a toothpick inserted in the center of a muffin comes out clean. Allow to sit 5 minutes before removing muffins from pan. Cool on a wire rack.

JO'S ROSEMARY BREAD

Servings: 12 | Prep: 10m | Cooks: 40m | Total: 3h | Additional: 2h10m

NUTRITION FACTS

Calories: 137 | Carbohydrates: 21.6g | Fat: 3.9g | Protein: 3.6g | Cholesterol: 0mg

INGREDIENTS

- 1 cup water
- 1/4 teaspoon ground black pepper
- 3 tablespoons olive oil

- 1 tablespoon dried rosemary
- 1 1/2 teaspoons white sugar
- 2 1/2 cups bread flour
- 1 1/2 teaspoons salt
- 1 1/2 teaspoons active dry yeast
- 1/4 teaspoon Italian seasoning

DIRECTIONS

1. Place ingredients in the pan of the bread machine in the order recommended by the manufacturer. Select white bread cycle; press Start.

CINNAMON ROLLS

Servings: 16 | Prep: 2h | Cooks: 20m | Total: 2h20m

NUTRITION FACTS

Calories: 372 | Carbohydrates: 45.2g | Fat: 19g | Protein: 6.4g | Cholesterol: 51mg

INGREDIENTS

- 1/4 cup water at room temperature
- 1/2 cup butter, softened
- 1/4 cup butter, melted
- 1 cup brown sugar
- 1/2 (3.4 ounce) package instant vanilla pudding mix
- 4 teaspoons ground cinnamon
- 1 cup warm milk
- 3/4 cup chopped pecans (optional)
- 1 egg, room temperature
- 1 (4 ounce) package cream cheese, softened
- 1 tablespoon white sugar
- 1/4 cup butter, softened
- 1/2 teaspoon salt
- 1 cup confectioners' sugar
- 4 cups bread flour
- 1/2 teaspoon vanilla extract
- 1 (.25 ounce) package active dry yeast
- 1 1/2 teaspoons milk

DIRECTIONS

1. In the pan of your bread machine, combine water, 1/4 cup melted butter, vanilla pudding, 1 cup warm milk, egg, 1 tablespoon sugar, salt, bread flour, and yeast. Set machine to Dough cycle; press Start.
2. When Dough cycle has finished, turn dough out onto a lightly floured surface and roll into a 17x10 inch rectangle. Spread with 1/2 cup softened butter. In a small bowl, stir together brown sugar, cinnamon, and pecans. Sprinkle brown sugar mixture over dough.
3. Butter a 9x13-inch baking pan.
4. Roll up dough, beginning with long side. Slice into 16 one-inch slices; place in prepared pan. Let rolls rise in a warm place until doubled, about 45 minutes.
5. Preheat oven to 350 degrees F (175 degrees C).
6. Bake rolls in preheated oven until browned, 15 to 20 minutes.
7. Stir together cream cheese, 1/4 cup softened butter, confectioners' sugar, vanilla extract, and 1 1/2 teaspoons milk. Remove rolls from oven and let cool until warm; spread frosting over warm rolls.

CINNAMON ROLLS

Servings: 6 | Prep: 15m | Cooks: 1h | Total: 1h15m

NUTRITION FACTS

Calories: 225 | Carbohydrates: 42.4g | Fat: 5.4g | Protein: 3g | Cholesterol: 31mg

INGREDIENTS

- 3 ripe bananas, mashed
- 1 1/2 cups all-purpose flour
- 1 cup white sugar
- 1 teaspoon baking soda
- 1 egg
- 1 teaspoon salt
- 1/4 cup melted butter

DIRECTIONS

1. Preheat oven to 325 degrees F (165 degrees C). Grease a 9x5-inch loaf pan.
2. Combine bananas, sugar, egg, and butter together in a bowl. Mix flour and baking soda together in a separate bowl; stir into banana mixture until batter is just mixed. Stir salt into batter. Pour batter into the prepared loaf pan.
3. Bake in the preheated oven until a toothpick inserted in the center of the bread comes out clean, about 1 hour.

BLUEBERRY CREAM MUFFINS

Servings: 24 | Prep: 10m | Cooks: 20m | Total: 30m

NUTRITION FACTS

Calories: 281 | Carbohydrates: 35.2g | Fat: 14.2g | Protein: 3.9g | Cholesterol: 39mg

INGREDIENTS

- 4 eggs
- 1 teaspoon salt
- 2 cups white sugar
- 1 teaspoon baking soda
- 1 cup vegetable oil
- 2 cups sour cream
- 1 teaspoon vanilla extract
- 2 cups blueberries
- 4 cups all-purpose flour

DIRECTIONS

1. Preheat oven to 400 degrees F (200 degrees C). Grease 24 muffin cups or line with paper muffin liners.
2. In large bowl beat eggs, gradually add sugar while beating. Continue beating while slowly pouring in oil. Stir in vanilla. In a separate bowl, stir together flour, salt and baking soda.
3. Stir dry ingredients into egg mixture alternately with sour cream. Gently fold in blueberries. Scoop batter into prepared muffin cups.
4. Bake in preheated oven for 20 minutes.

CLASSIC BRAN MUFFINS

Servings: 12 | Prep: 20m | Cooks: 20m | Total: 40m

NUTRITION FACTS

Calories: 167 | Carbohydrates: 3.5g | Fat: 7.1g | Protein: 3.5g | Cholesterol: 16mg

INGREDIENTS

- 1 1/2 cups wheat bran
- 1 cup all-purpose flour
- 1 cup buttermilk

- 1 teaspoon baking soda
- 1/3 cup vegetable oil
- 1 teaspoon baking powder
- 1 egg
- 1/2 teaspoon salt
- 2/3 cup brown sugar
- 1/2 cup raisins
- 1/2 teaspoon vanilla extract

DIRECTIONS

1. Preheat oven to 375 degrees F (190 degrees C). Grease muffin cups or line with paper muffin liners.
2. Mix together wheat bran and buttermilk; let stand for 10 minutes.
3. Beat together oil, egg, sugar and vanilla and add to buttermilk/bran mixture. Sift together flour, baking soda, baking powder and salt. Stir flour mixture into buttermilk mixture, until just blended. Fold in raisins and spoon batter into prepared muffin tins.
4. Bake for 15 to 20 minutes, or until a toothpick inserted into the center of a muffin comes out clean. Cool and enjoy.

FRENCH BAGUETTES

Servings: 12 | Prep: 15m | Cooks: 25m | Total: 1h50m | Additional: 1h10m

NUTRITION FACTS

Calories: 113 | Carbohydrates: 22g | Fat: 0.9g | Protein: 3.8g | Cholesterol: 17mg

INGREDIENTS

- 1 cup water
- 1 1/2 teaspoons bread machine yeast
- 2 1/2 cups bread flour
- 1 egg yolk
- 1 tablespoon white sugar
- 1 tablespoon water
- 1 teaspoon salt

DIRECTIONS

1. Place 1 cup water, bread flour, sugar, salt and yeast into bread machine pan in the order recommended by manufacturer. Select Dough cycle, and press Start.
2. When the cycle has completed, place dough in a greased bowl, turning to coat all sides. Cover, and let rise in a warm place for about 30 minutes, or until doubled in bulk. Dough is ready if indentation remains when touched.
3. Punch down dough. On a lightly floured surface, roll into a 16x12 inch rectangle. Cut dough in half, creating two 8x12 inch rectangles. Roll up each half of dough tightly, beginning at 12 inch side, pounding out any air bubbles as you go. Roll gently back and forth to taper end. Place 3 inches apart on a greased cookie sheet. Make deep diagonal slashes across loaves every 2 inches, or make one lengthwise slash on each loaf. Cover, and let rise in a warm place for 30 to 40 minutes, or until doubled in bulk.
4. Preheat oven to 375 degrees F (190 degrees C). Mix egg yolk with 1 tablespoon water; brush over tops of loaves.
5. Bake for 20 to 25 minutes in the preheated oven, or until golden brown.

THE BEST BANANA BREAD
Servings: 15 | Prep: 15m | Cooks: 1h | Total: 1h15m

NUTRITION FACTS

Calories: 196 | Carbohydrates: 31.3g | Fat: 7g | Protein: 2.9g | Cholesterol: 25mg

INGREDIENTS

- 1/2 cup margarine, softened
- 1 1/2 cups mashed banana
- 1 cup white sugar
- 2 cups all-purpose flour
- 2 eggs
- 1 teaspoon baking soda

DIRECTIONS

1. Preheat oven to 350 degrees F (175 degrees C). Grease and flour one 9x5 inch pan.
2. Cream margarine and sugar until smooth. Beat in eggs, then bananas. Add flour and soda, stirring just until combined.
3. Pour into prepared pan and bake at 350 degrees F (175 degrees C) for about 1 hour (or till toothpick comes out clean). Remove from pan and let cool, store in refrigerator or freeze.

QUICK YEAST ROLLS
Servings: 8 | Prep: 1h30m | Cooks: 10m | Total: 1h40m

NUTRITION FACTS

Calories: 186 | Carbohydrates: 31.9g | Fat: 4.2g | Protein: 4.8g | Cholesterol: 23mg

INGREDIENTS

- 2 tablespoons shortening
- 1 egg, beaten
- 3 tablespoons white sugar
- 1 teaspoon salt
- 1 cup hot water
- 2 1/4 cups all-purpose flour
- 1 (.25 ounce) package active dry yeast

DIRECTIONS

1. In a large bowl, mix the shortening, sugar, and hot water. Allow to cool until lukewarm, and mix in the yeast until dissolved. Mix in the egg, salt, and flour. Allow the dough to rise until doubled in size.
2. Grease 8 muffin cups. Divide the dough into the prepared muffin cups, and allow to rise again until doubled in size.
3. Preheat oven to 425 degrees F (220 degrees C).
4. Bake for 10 minutes in the preheated oven, or until a knife inserted in the center of a muffin comes out clean.

BANANA BREAD

Servings: 16 | Prep: 15m | Cooks: 1h | Total: 1h15m

NUTRITION FACTS

Calories: 145 | Carbohydrates: 26.5g | Fat: 3.7g | Protein: 2.3g | Cholesterol: 31mg

INGREDIENTS

1 1/2 cups all-purpose flour

2 eggs, beaten

1 teaspoon baking soda

1/4 cup butter, melted

1/2 teaspoon salt

3 bananas, mashed

1 cup white sugar

DIRECTIONS

1. Grease and flour two 7x3 inch loaf pans. Preheat oven to 350 degrees F (175 degrees C).
2. In one bowl, whisk together flour, soda, salt, and sugar. Mix in slightly beaten eggs, melted butter, and mashed bananas. Stir in nuts if desired. Pour into prepared pans.
3. Bake at 350 degrees F (175 degrees C) for 1 hour, or until a wooden toothpick inserted in the center comes out clean.

MALL PRETZELS

Servings: 12 | Prep: 30m | Cooks: 20m | Total: 3h | Additional: 2h10m

NUTRITION FACTS

Calories: 182 | Carbohydrates: 34.6g | Fat: 2.4g | Protein: 4.8g | Cholesterol: 5mg

INGREDIENTS

- 1 (.25 ounce) package active dry yeast
- 1 cup bread flour
- 2 tablespoons brown sugar
- 2 cups warm water (110 degrees F/45 degrees C)
- 1 1/8 teaspoons salt
- 2 tablespoons baking soda
- 1 1/2 cups warm water (110 degrees F/45 degrees C)
- 2 tablespoons butter, melted
- 3 cups all-purpose flour
- 2 tablespoons coarse kosher salt

DIRECTIONS

1. In a large mixing bowl, dissolve the yeast, brown sugar and salt in 1 1/2 cups warm water. Stir in flour, and knead dough on a floured surface until smooth and elastic, about 8 minutes. Place in a greased bowl, and turn to coat the surface. Cover, and let rise for one hour.
2. Combine 2 cups warm water and baking soda in an 8 inch square pan. Line 6 baking sheets with parchment paper.

3. After dough has risen, cut into 12 pieces. Roll each piece into a 3 foot rope, pencil thin or thinner. Twist into a pretzel shape, and dip into the baking soda solution. Place onto parchment covered baking sheets, and let rise 15 to 20 minutes.
4. Preheat an oven to 450 degrees F (230 degrees C).
5. Bake in the preheated oven for 8 to 10 minutes, or until golden brown. Brush with melted butter, and sprinkle with coarse salt, garlic salt or cinnamon sugar.

AMAZINGLY EASY IRISH SODA BREAD
Servings: 20 | Prep: 15m | Cooks: 50m | Total: 1h5m

NUTRITION FACTS

Calories: 172 | Carbohydrates: 22.5g | Fat: 7.5g | Protein: 3.5g | Cholesterol: 16mg

INGREDIENTS

- 4 cups all-purpose flour
- 1/2 cup margarine, softened
- 4 tablespoons white sugar
- 1 cup buttermilk
- 1 teaspoon baking soda
- 1 egg
- 1 tablespoon baking powder
- 1/4 cup butter, melted
- 1/2 teaspoon salt
- 1/4 cup buttermilk

DIRECTIONS

1. Preheat oven to 375 degrees F (190 degrees C). Lightly grease a large baking sheet.
2. In a large bowl, mix together flour, sugar, baking soda, baking powder, salt and margarine. Stir in 1 cup of buttermilk and egg. Turn dough out onto a lightly floured surface and knead slightly. Form dough into a round and place on prepared baking sheet. In a small bowl, combine melted butter with 1/4 cup buttermilk; brush loaf with this mixture. Use a sharp knife to cut an 'X' into the top of the loaf.
3. Bake in preheated oven until a toothpick inserted into the center of the loaf comes out clean, 45 to 50 minutes. Check for doneness after 30 minutes. You may continue to brush the loaf with the butter mixture while it bakes.

FRENCH BREAD ROLLS TO DIE FOR
Servings: 16 | Prep: 20m | Cooks: 20m | Total: 2h20m | Additional: 1h40m

NUTRITION FACTS

Calories: | Carbohydrates: g | Fat: g | Protein: g | Cholesterol: mg

INGREDIENTS

- 1 1/2 cups warm water (110 degrees F/45 degrees C)
- 2 tablespoons vegetable oil
- 1 tablespoon active dry yeast
- 1 teaspoon salt
- 2 tablespoons white sugar
- 4 cups bread flour

DIRECTIONS

1. In a large bowl, stir together warm water, yeast, and sugar. Let stand until creamy, about 10 minutes.
2. To the yeast mixture, add the oil, salt, and 2 cups flour. Stir in the remaining flour, 1/2 cup at a time, until the dough has pulled away from the sides of the bowl. Turn out onto a lightly floured surface, and knead until smooth and elastic, about 8 minutes. Lightly oil a large bowl, place the dough in the bowl, and turn to coat. Cover with a damp cloth, and let rise in a warm place until doubled in volume, about 1 hour.
3. Deflate the dough, and turn it out onto a lightly floured surface. Divide the dough into 16 equal pieces, and form into round balls. Place on lightly greased baking sheets at least 2 inches apart. Cover the rolls with a damp cloth, and let rise until doubled in volume, about 40 minutes. Meanwhile, preheat oven to 400 degrees F (200 degrees C).
4. Bake for 18 to 20 minutes in the preheated oven, or until golden brown.

PUMPKIN GINGERBREAD

Servings: 6 | Prep: 15m | Cooks: 45m | Total: 1h

NUTRITION FACTS

Calories: 263 | Carbohydrates: 40.7g | Fat: 10.2g | Protein: 3.2g | Cholesterol: 31mg

INGREDIENTS

- 3 cups sugar
- 1 teaspoon ground cinnamon
- 1 cup vegetable oil
- 1 teaspoon ground cloves
- 4 eggs

- 3 1/2 cups all-purpose flour
- 2/3 cup water
- 2 teaspoons baking soda
- 1 (15 ounce) can pumpkin puree
- 1 1/2 teaspoons salt
- 2 teaspoons ground ginger
- 1/2 teaspoon baking powder
- 1 teaspoon ground allspice
- 1 teaspoon ground cinnamon

DIRECTIONS

1. Preheat oven to 350 degrees F (175 degrees C). Lightly grease two 9x5 inch loaf pans.
2. In a large mixing, combine sugar, oil and eggs; beat until smooth. Add water and beat until well blended. Stir in pumpkin, ginger, allspice cinnamon, and clove.
3. In medium bowl, combine flour, soda, salt, and baking powder. Add dry ingredients to pumpkin mixture and blend just until all ingredients are mixed. Divide batter between prepared pans.
4. Bake in preheated oven until toothpick comes out clean, about 1 hour.

BANANA OAT MUFFINS

Servings: 12 | Prep: 15m | Cooks: 20m | Total: 35m

NUTRITION FACTS

Calories: 200 | Carbohydrates: 30.1g | Fat: 7.5g | Protein: 3.7g | Cholesterol: 17mg

INGREDIENTS

- 1 1/2 cups unbleached all-purpose flour
- 1 egg
- 1 cup rolled oats
- 3/4 cup milk
- 1/2 cup white sugar
- 1/3 cup vegetable oil
- 2 teaspoons baking powder
- 1/2 teaspoon vanilla extract
- 1 teaspoon baking soda
- 1 cup mashed bananas
- 1/2 teaspoon salt

DIRECTIONS

1. Combine flour, oats, sugar, baking powder, soda, and salt.
2. In a large bowl, beat the egg lightly. Stir in the milk, oil, and vanilla. Add the mashed banana, and combine thoroughly. Stir the flour mixture into the banana mixture until just combined. Line a 12-cup muffin tin with paper bake cups, and divide the batter among them.
3. Bake at 400 degrees F (205 degrees C) for 18 to 20 minutes.

PIZZA DOUGH

Servings: 12 | Prep: 15m | Cooks: 20m | Total: 1h5m | Additional: 30m

NUTRITION FACTS

Calories: 24 | Carbohydrates: 0.9g | Fat: 2.3g | Protein: 0.2g | Cholesterol: 0mg

INGREDIENTS

- 1 (.25 ounce) package active dry yeast
- 2 tablespoons olive oil
- 1 cup warm water (110 degrees F/45 degrees C)
- 1 teaspoon salt
- 2 cups bread flour
- 2 teaspoons white sugar

DIRECTIONS

1. In a small bowl, dissolve yeast in warm water. Let stand until creamy, about 10 minutes.
2. In a large bowl, combine 2 cups bread flour, olive oil, salt, white sugar and the yeast mixture; stir well to combine. Beat well until a stiff dough has formed. Cover and rise until doubled in volume, about 30 minutes. Meanwhile, preheat oven to 350 degrees F (175 degrees C).
3. Turn dough out onto a well floured surface. Form dough into a round and roll out into a pizza crust shape. Cover with your favorite sauce and toppings and bake in preheated oven until golden brown, about 20 minutes.

DUMPLINGS

Servings: 6 | Prep: 5m | Cooks: 15m | Total: 20m

NUTRITION FACTS

Calories: 105 | Carbohydrates: 18g | Fat: 2.4g | Protein: 2.8g | Cholesterol: 2mg

INGREDIENTS

- 1 cup all-purpose flour
- 1/2 teaspoon salt
- 2 teaspoons baking powder
- 1 tablespoon margarine
- 1 teaspoon white sugar
- 1/2 cup milk

DIRECTIONS

1. Stir together flour, baking powder, sugar, and salt in medium size bowl. Cut in butter until crumbly. Stir in milk to make a soft dough.
2. Drop by spoonfuls into boiling stew. Cover and simmer 15 minutes without lifting lid. Serve.
3. To make parsley dumplings, add 1 tablespoon parsley flakes to the dry ingredients.

PUMPKIN CHOCOLATE CHIP MUFFINS
Servings: 12 | Prep: 10m | Cooks: 20m | Total: 30m

NUTRITION FACTS

Calories: 197 | Carbohydrates: 30.4g | Fat: 7.7g | Protein: 3.1g | Cholesterol: 31mg

INGREDIENTS

- 3/4 cup white sugar
- 1/2 teaspoon baking soda
- 1/4 cup vegetable oil
- 1/4 teaspoon ground cloves
- 2 eggs
- 1/2 teaspoon ground cinnamon
- 3/4 cup canned pumpkin
- 1/4 teaspoon salt
- 1/4 cup water
- 1/4 teaspoon ground nutmeg
- 1 1/2 cups all-purpose flour
- 1/2 cup semisweet chocolate chips
- 3/4 teaspoon baking powder

DIRECTIONS

1. Preheat the oven to 400 degrees F (200 degrees C). Grease and flour muffin pan or use paper liners.
2. Mix sugar, oil, eggs. Add pumpkin and water. In separate bowl mix together the baking flour, baking soda, baking powder, spices and salt. Add wet mixture and stir in chocolate chips.
3. Fill muffin cups 2/3 full with batter. Bake in preheated oven for 20 to 25 minutes.

HOMEMADE FLOUR TORTILLAS

Servings: 24 | Prep: 15m | Cooks: 45m | Total: 1h

NUTRITION FACTS

Calories: 86 | Carbohydrates: 16g | Fat: 1.3g | Protein: 2.2g | Cholesterol: 1mg

INGREDIENTS

- 4 cups all-purpose flour
- 2 tablespoons lard
- 1 teaspoon salt
- 1 1/2 cups water
- 2 teaspoons baking powder

DIRECTIONS

1. Whisk the flour, salt, and baking powder together in a mixing bowl. Mix in the lard with your fingers until the flour resembles cornmeal. Add the water and mix until the dough comes together; place on a lightly floured surface and knead a few minutes until smooth and elastic. Divide the dough into 24 equal pieces and roll each piece into a ball.
2. Preheat a large skillet over medium-high heat. Use a well-floured rolling pin to roll a dough ball into a thin, round tortilla. Place into the hot skillet, and cook until bubbly and golden; flip and continue cooking until golden on the other side. Place the cooked tortilla in a tortilla warmer; continue rolling and cooking the remaining dough.

FOCACCIA BREAD

Servings: 12 | Prep: 20m | Cooks: 15m | Total: 1h | Additional: 25m

NUTRITION FACTS

Calories: 171 | Carbohydrates: 23.4g | Fat: 5.8g | Protein: 6g | Cholesterol: 5mg

INGREDIENTS

- 2 3/4 cups all-purpose flour
- 1/2 teaspoon dried basil
- 1 teaspoon salt
- 1 pinch ground black pepper
- 1 teaspoon white sugar
- 1 tablespoon vegetable oil
- 1 tablespoon active dry yeast
- 1 cup water
- 1 teaspoon garlic powder
- 2 tablespoons olive oil
- 1 teaspoon dried oregano
- 1 tablespoon grated Parmesan cheese
- 1 teaspoon dried thyme
- 1 cup mozzarella

DIRECTIONS

1. In a large bowl, stir together the flour, salt, sugar, yeast, garlic powder, oregano, thyme, basil and black pepper. Mix in the vegetable oil and water.
2. When the dough has pulled together, turn it out onto a lightly floured surface, and knead until smooth and elastic. Lightly oil a large bowl, place the dough in the bowl, and turn to coat with oil. Cover with a damp cloth, and let rise in a warm place for 20 minutes.
3. Preheat oven to 450 degrees F (230 degrees C). Punch dough down; place on greased baking sheet. Pat into a 1/2 inch thick rectangle. Brush top with olive oil. Sprinkle with Parmesan cheese and mozzarella cheese.
4. Bake in preheated oven for 15 minutes, or until golden brown. Serve warm.

IRRESISTIBLE IRISH SODA BREAD
Servings: 12 | Prep: 15m | Cooks: 1h10m | Total: 1h25m

NUTRITION FACTS

Calories: 192 | Carbohydrates: 31.7g | Fat: 4.9g | Protein: 5.1g | Cholesterol: 27mg

INGREDIENTS

- 3 cups all-purpose flour
- 1 teaspoon baking soda
- 1 tablespoon baking powder
- 1 egg, lightly beaten

- 1/3 cup white sugar
- 2 cups buttermilk
- 1 teaspoon salt
- 1/4 cup butter, melted

DIRECTIONS

1. Preheat oven to 325 degrees F (165 degrees C). Grease a 9x5 inch loaf pan.
2. Combine flour, baking powder, sugar, salt and baking soda. Blend egg and buttermilk together, and add all at once to the flour mixture. Mix just until moistened. Stir in butter. Pour into prepared pan.
3. Bake for 65 to 70 minutes, or until a toothpick inserted in the bread comes out clean. Cool on a wire rack. Wrap in foil for several hours, or overnight, for best flavor.

CRISPY AND CREAMY DOUGHNUTS

Servings: 18 | Prep: 10m | Cooks: 30m | Total: 2h40m | Additional: 2h

NUTRITION FACTS

Calories: 330 | Carbohydrates: 47.3g | Fat: 13.4g | Protein: 5.3g | Cholesterol: 31mg

INGREDIENTS

- 2 (.25 ounce) envelopes active dry yeast
- 5 cups all-purpose flour
- 1/4 cup warm water (105 to 115 degrees)
- 1 quart vegetable oil for frying
- 1 1/2 cups lukewarm milk
- 1/3 cup butter
- 1/2 cup white sugar
- 2 cups confectioners' sugar
- 1 teaspoon salt
- 1 1/2 teaspoons vanilla
- 2 eggs
- 4 tablespoons hot water or as needed
- 1/3 cup shortening

DIRECTIONS

1. Sprinkle the yeast over the warm water, and let stand for 5 minutes, or until foamy.

2. In a large bowl, mix together the yeast mixture, milk, sugar, salt, eggs, shortening, and 2 cups of the flour. Mix for a few minutes at low speed, or stirring with a wooden spoon. Beat in remaining flour 1/2 cup at a time, until the dough no longer sticks to the bowl. Knead for about 5 minutes, or until smooth and elastic. Place the dough into a greased bowl, and cover. Set in a warm place to rise until double. Dough is ready if you touch it, and the indention remains.

3. Turn the dough out onto a floured surface, and gently roll out to 1/2 inch thickness. Cut with a floured doughnut cutter. Let doughnuts sit out to rise again until double. Cover loosely with a cloth.

4. Melt butter in a saucepan over medium heat. Stir in confectioners' sugar and vanilla until smooth. Remove from heat, and stir in hot water one tablespoon at a time until the icing is somewhat thin, but not watery. Set aside.

5. Heat oil in a deep-fryer or large heavy skillet to 350 degrees F (175 degrees C). Slide doughnuts into the hot oil using a wide spatula. Turn doughnuts over as they rise to the surface. Fry doughnuts on each side until golden brown. Remove from hot oil, to drain on a wire rack. Dip doughnuts into the glaze while still hot, and set onto wire racks to drain off excess. Keep a cookie sheet or tray under racks for easier clean up.

ABSOLUTE MEXICAN CORNBREAD

Servings: 6 | Prep: 15m | Cooks: 1h | Total: 1h15m

NUTRITION FACTS

Calories: 743 | Carbohydrates: 83.6g | Fat: 40.9g | Protein: 14.5g | Cholesterol: 22.4mg

INGREDIENTS

- 1 cup butter, melted
- 1/2 cup shredded Cheddar cheese
- 1 cup white sugar
- 1 cup all-purpose flour
- 4 eggs
- 1 cup yellow cornmeal
- 1 (15 ounce) can cream-style corn
- 4 teaspoons baking powder
- 1/2 (4 ounce) can chopped green chile peppers, drained
- ¼ teaspoon salt
- 1/2 cup shredded Monterey Jack cheese

DIRECTIONS

1. In a large bowl, beat together butter and sugar. Beat in eggs one at a time. Blend in cream corn, chiles, Monterey Jack and Cheddar cheese.
2. In a separate bowl, stir together flour, cornmeal, baking powder and salt. Add flour mixture to corn mixture; stir until smooth. Pour batter into prepared pan.
3. Bake in preheated oven for 1 hour, until a toothpick inserted into center of the pan comes out clean.

OOEY-GOOEY CINNAMON BUNS

Servings: 15 | Prep: 2h30m | Cooks: 0m | Total: 3h

NUTRITION FACTS

Calories: 392 | Carbohydrates: 45.3g | Fat: 21.7g | Protein: 5.6g | Cholesterol: 66mg

INGREDIENTS

- 1 teaspoon white sugar
- 2 eggs, beaten
- 1 (.25 ounce) package active dry yeast
- 4 cups all-purpose flour
- 1/2 cup warm water (110 degrees F/45 degrees C)
- 3/4 cup butter
- 1/2 cup milk
- 3/4 cup brown sugar
- 1/4 cup white sugar
- 1 cup chopped pecans, divided
- 1/4 cup butter
- 3/4 cup brown sugar
- 1 teaspoon salt
- 1 tablespoon ground cinnamon
- 1/4 cup melted butter

DIRECTIONS

1. In a small bowl, dissolve 1 teaspoon sugar and yeast in warm water. Let stand until creamy, about 10 minutes. Warm the milk in a small saucepan until it bubbles, then remove from heat. Mix in 1/4 cup sugar, 1/4 cup butter and salt; stir until melted. Let cool until lukewarm.
2. In a large bowl, combine the yeast mixture, milk mixture, eggs and 1 1/2 cup flour; stir well to combine. Stir in the remaining flour, 1/2 cup at a time, beating well after each addition. When the dough has pulled together, turn it out onto a lightly floured surface and knead until smooth and elastic, about 8 minutes.

3. Lightly oil a large bowl, place the dough in the bowl and turn to coat with oil. Cover with a damp cloth and let rise in a warm place until doubled in volume, about 1 hour.

4. While dough is rising, melt 3/4 cup butter in a small saucepan over medium heat. Stir in 3/4 cup brown sugar, whisking until smooth. Pour into greased 9x13 inch baking pan. Sprinkle bottom of pan with 1/2 cup pecans; set aside. Melt remaining butter; set aside. Combine remaining 3/4 cup brown sugar, 1/2 cup pecans, and cinnamon; set aside.

5. Turn dough out onto a lightly floured surface, roll into an 18x14 inch rectangle. Brush with 2 tablespoons melted butter, leaving 1/2 inch border uncovered; sprinkle with brown sugar cinnamon mixture. Starting at long side, tightly roll up, pinching seam to seal. Brush with remaining 2 tablespoons butter. With serrated knife, cut into 15 pieces; place cut side down, in prepared pan. Cover and let rise for 1 hour or until doubled in volume. Meanwhile, preheat oven to 375 degrees F (190 degrees C).

6. Bake in preheated oven for 25 to 30 minutes, until golden brown. Let cool in pan for 3 minutes, then invert onto serving platter. Scrape remaining filling from the pan onto the rolls.

FRENCH BREAD

Servings: 30 | Prep: 25 | Cooks: 40m | Total: 2h40m | Additional: 1h35m

NUTRITION FACTS

Calories: 94 | Carbohydrates: 19.5g | Fat: 0.3g | Protein: 2.9g | Cholesterol: 0mg

INGREDIENTS

- 6 cups all-purpose flour
- 1 tablespoon cornmeal
- 2 1/2 (.25 ounce) packages active dry yeast
- 1 egg white
- 1 1/2 teaspoons salt
- 1 tablespoon water
- 2 cups warm water (110 degrees F/45 degrees C)

DIRECTIONS

1. In a large bowl, combine 2 cups flour, yeast and salt. Stir in 2 cups warm water, and beat until well blended using a stand mixer with a dough hook attachment. Using a wooden spoon, stir in as much of the remaining flour as you can.

2. On a lightly floured surface, knead in enough flour to make a stiff dough that is smooth and elastic. Knead for about 8 to 10 minutes total. Shape into a ball. Place dough in a greased bowl, and turn once. Cover, and let rise in a warm place until doubled.

3. Punch dough down, and divide in half. Turn out onto a lightly floured surface. Cover, and let rest for 10 minutes. Roll each half into large rectangle. Roll up, starting from a long side. Moisten edge with water and seal. Taper ends.
4. Grease a large baking sheet. Sprinkle with cornmeal. Place loaves, seam side down, on the prepared baking sheet. Lightly beat the egg white with 1 tablespoon of water, and brush on. Cover with a damp cloth. Let rise until nearly doubled, 35 to 40 minutes.
5. With a very sharp knife, make 3 or 4 diagonal cuts about 1/4 inch deep across top of each loaf. Bake in a preheated 375 degrees F (190 degrees C) oven for 20 minutes. Brush again with egg white mixture. Bake for an additional 15 to 20 minutes, or until bread tests done. If necessary, cover loosely with foil to prevent over browning. Remove from baking sheet, and cool on a wire rack.

CHOCOLATE BANANA BREAD

Servings: 24 | Prep: 10m | Cooks: 1h | Total: 1h10m

NUTRITION FACTS

Calories: 278 | Carbohydrates: 40.8 | Fat: 12.1g | Protein: 3.8g | Cholesterol: 35mg

INGREDIENTS

- 1 cup margarine, softened
- 3 cups all-purpose flour
- 2 cups white sugar
- 2 teaspoons baking soda
- 4 eggs
- 1/4 cup unsweetened cocoa powder
- 6 bananas, mashed
- 1 cup lite sour cream
- 2 teaspoons vanilla extract
- 1 cup semisweet chocolate chips

DIRECTIONS

1. Preheat oven to 350 degrees F (175 degrees C). Lightly grease two 9x5 inch loaf pans.
2. In a large bowl, cream together margarine, sugar and eggs. Stir in bananas and vanilla. Sift in flour, baking soda and cocoa; mix well. Blend in sour cream and chocolate chips. Pour batter into prepared pans.
3. Bake in preheated oven for 60 minutes, or until a toothpick inserted into center of a loaf comes out clean.

CATHY'S BANANA BREAD

Servings: 16 | Prep: 10m | Cooks: 50m | Total: 1h

NUTRITION FACTS

Calories: 200 | Carbohydrates: 32.6g | Fat: 6.6g | Protein: 3g | Cholesterol: 30mg

INGREDIENTS

- 1 cup mashed bananas
- 1 teaspoon vanilla extract
- 1 cup sour cream
- 2 cups all-purpose flour
- 1/4 cup margarine
- 1 teaspoon baking soda
- 1 1/3 cups white sugar
- 1 teaspoon baking powder
- 2 eggs
- 1/4 teaspoon salt

DIRECTIONS

1. Preheat oven to 350 degrees F (175 degrees C). Grease and flour one 9x13 inch pan, or two 7x3 inch loaf pans.
2. Combine banana and sour cream. Set aside. In a large bowl, cream together the margarine and sugar until smooth. Beat in the eggs one at a time, then stir in the vanilla and banana mixture. Combine the flour, baking soda, baking powder and salt; stir into the banana mixture. Spread the batter evenly into the prepared pan or pans.
3. Bake for 50 minutes in the preheated oven, or until a toothpick inserted into the center of the bread comes out clean.

SCONES

Servings: 8 | Prep: 10m | Cooks: 15m | Total: 25m

NUTRITION FACTS

Calories: 397 | Carbohydrates: 50.6g | Fat: 18.9g | Protein: 6.8g | Cholesterol: 71mg

INGREDIENTS

- 3 cups all-purpose flour
- 3/4 cup butter
- 1/2 cup white sugar
- 1 egg, beaten
- 5 teaspoons baking powder
- 1 cup milk
- 1/2 teaspoon salt

DIRECTIONS

1. Preheat oven to 400 degrees F (200 degrees C). Lightly grease a baking sheet.
2. In a large bowl, combine flour, sugar, baking powder, and salt. Cut in butter. Mix the egg and milk in a small bowl, and stir into flour mixture until moistened.
3. Turn dough out onto a lightly floured surface, and knead briefly. Roll dough out into a 1/2 inch thick round. Cut into 8 wedges, and place on the prepared baking sheet.
4. Bake 15 minutes in the preheated oven, or until golden brown.

CHEF JOHN'S BUTTERMILK BISCUITS

Servings: 12 | Prep: 20m | Cooks: 15m | Total: 35m

NUTRITION FACTS

Calories: 143 | Carbohydrates: 17g | Fat: 7.1g | Protein: 2.8g | Cholesterol: 19mg

INGREDIENTS

- 2 cups all-purpose flour
- 7 tablespoons unsalted butter, chilled in freezer and cut into thin slices
- 2 teaspoons baking powder
- 3/4 cup cold buttermilk
- 1 teaspoon salt
- 2 tablespoons buttermilk for brushing
- 1/4 teaspoon baking soda

DIRECTIONS

1. Preheat oven to 425 degrees F (220 degrees C).
2. Line a baking sheet with a silicone baking mat or parchment paper.
3. Whisk flour, baking powder, salt, and baking soda together in a large bowl.

4. Cut butter into flour mixture with a pastry blender until the mixture resembles coarse crumbs, about 5 minutes.
5. Make a well in the center of butter and flour mixture. Pour in 3/4 cup buttermilk; stir until just combined.
6. Turn dough onto a floured work surface, pat together into a rectangle.
7. Fold the rectangle in thirds. Turn dough a half turn, gather any crumbs, and flatten back into a rectangle. Repeat twice more, folding and pressing dough a total of three times.
8. Roll dough on a floured surface to about 1/2 inch thick.
9. Cut out 12 biscuits using a 2 1/2-inch round biscuit cutter.
10. Transfer biscuits to the prepared baking sheet. Press an indent into the top of each biscuit with your thumb.
11. Brush the tops of biscuits with 2 tablespoons buttermilk.
12. Bake in the preheated oven until browned, about 15 minutes.

E-Z DROP BISCUITS

Servings: 12 | Prep: 15m | Cooks: 15m | Total: 30m

NUTRITION FACTS

Calories: 157 | Carbohydrates: 17.8g | Fat: 8.3g | Protein: 2.9g | Cholesterol: 22mg

INGREDIENTS

- 2 cups all-purpose flour
- 1/4 teaspoon salt
- 1 tablespoon baking powder
- 1/2 cup melted butter
- 2 teaspoons white sugar
- 1 cup milk
- 1/2 teaspoon cream of tartar

DIRECTIONS

1. Preheat oven to 450 degrees F (230 degrees C).
2. In a large bowl, combine flour, baking powder, sugar, cream of tartar and salt. Stir in butter and milk just until moistened. Drop batter on a lightly greased cookie sheet by the tablespoon.
3. Bake in preheated oven until golden on the edges, about 8 to 12 minutes. Serve warm.

STRAWBERRY BREAD

Servings: 24 | Prep: 30m | Cooks: 45m | Total: 1h25m | Additional: 10m

NUTRITION FACTS

Calories: 281 | Carbohydrates: 31.2g | Fat: 16.6g | Protein: 3.3g | Cholesterol: 31mg

INGREDIENTS

- 2 cups fresh strawberries
- 1 teaspoon baking soda
- 3 1/8 cups all-purpose flour
- 1 1/4 cups vegetable oil
- 2 cups white sugar
- 4 eggs, beaten
- 1 tablespoon ground cinnamon
- 1 1/4 cups chopped pecans
- 1 teaspoon salt

DIRECTIONS

1. Preheat oven to 350 degrees F (175 degrees C). Butter and flour two 9 x 5-inch loaf pans.
2. Slice strawberries and place in medium-sized bowl. Sprinkle lightly with sugar, and set aside while preparing batter.
3. Combine flour, sugar, cinnamon, salt and baking soda in large bowl; mix well. Blend oil and eggs into strawberries. Add strawberry mixture to flour mixture, blending until dry ingredients are just moistened. Stir in pecans. Divide batter into pans.
4. Bake in preheated oven until a tester inserted in the center comes out clean, 45 to 50 minutes (test each loaf separately). Let cool in pans on wire rack for 10 minutes. Turn loaves out of pans, and allow to cool before slicing.

PUMPKIN APPLE STREUSEL MUFFINS

Servings: 18 | Prep: 15m | Cooks: 45m | Total: 1h

NUTRITION FACTS

Calories: 249 | Carbohydrates: 42.6g | Fat: 8g | Protein: 2.8g | Cholesterol: 23mg

INGREDIENTS

- 2 1/2 cups all-purpose flour
- 1/2 cup vegetable oil
- 2 cups white sugar
- 2 cups peeled, cored and chopped apple
- 1 tablespoon pumpkin pie spice

* 2 tablespoons all-purpose flour
* 1 teaspoon baking soda
* 1/4 cup white sugar
* 1/2 teaspoon salt
* 1/2 teaspoon ground cinnamon
* 2 eggs, lightly beaten
* 4 teaspoons butter
* 1 cup canned pumpkin puree

DIRECTIONS

1. Preheat oven to 350 degrees F (175 degrees C). Lightly grease 18 muffin cups or use paper liners.
2. In a large bowl, sift together 2 1/2 cups all-purpose flour, 2 cups sugar, pumpkin pie spice, baking soda and salt. In a separate bowl, mix together eggs, pumpkin and oil. Add pumpkin mixture to flour mixture; stirring just to moisten. Fold in apples. Spoon batter into prepared muffin cups.
3. In a small bowl, mix together 2 tablespoons flour, 1/4 cup sugar and 1/2 teaspoon cinnamon. Cut in butter until mixture resembles coarse crumbs. Sprinkle topping evenly over muffin batter.
4. Bake in preheated oven for 35 to 40 minutes, or until a toothpick inserted into a muffin comes out clean.

4H BANANA BREAD

Servings: 12 | Prep: 10m | Cooks: 1h | Total: 1h10m

NUTRITION FACTS

Calories: 265 | Carbohydrates: 38g | Fat: 11.5g | Protein: 3.9g | Cholesterol: 16mg

INGREDIENTS

* 2 cups all-purpose flour
* 1 teaspoon baking powder
* 1/2 teaspoon baking soda
* 1/2 teaspoon salt
* 1 cup white sugar
* 1/2 cup margarine
* 1 egg
* 1 cup mashed bananas
* 5 tablespoons milk

- 1/2 cup chopped walnuts (optional)

DIRECTIONS

1. Sift together flour, baking soda, baking powder, and salt.
2. In a large bowl, cream sugar and butter or margarine. Beat the egg slightly, and mix into the creamed mixture with the bananas. Mix in sifted ingredients until just combined. Stir in milk and nuts. Spread batter into one greased and floured 9x5 inch loaf pan.
3. Bake at 350 degrees F (175 degrees C) until top is brown and cracks along the top.

CINNAMON BREAD

Servings: 12 | Prep: 20m | Cooks: 50m | Total: 1h10m

NUTRITION FACTS

Calories: 218 | Carbohydrates: 36.4g | Fat: 6.4g | Protein: 3.9g | Cholesterol: 32mg

INGREDIENTS

- 2 cups all-purpose flour
- 1 cup buttermilk
- 1 cup white sugar
- 1/4 cup vegetable oil
- 2 teaspoons baking powder
- 2 eggs
- 1/2 teaspoon baking soda
- 2 teaspoons vanilla extract
- 1 1/2 teaspoons ground cinnamon
- 2 tablespoons white sugar
- 1 teaspoon salt
- 1 teaspoon ground cinnamon
- 2 teaspoons margarine

DIRECTIONS

1. Preheat oven to 350 degrees F (175 degrees C). Grease one 9x5 inch loaf pan.
2. Measure flour, 1 cup sugar, baking powder, baking soda, 1 1/2 teaspoons cinnamon, salt, buttermilk, oil, eggs and vanilla into large mixing bowl. Beat 3 minutes. Pour into prepared loaf pan. Smooth top.

3. Combine 2 tablespoons white sugar, 1 teaspoon cinnamon and butter, mixing until crumbly. Sprinkle topping over smoothed batter. Using knife, cut in a light swirling motion to give a marbled effect.
4. Bake for about 50 minutes. Test with toothpick. When inserted it should come out clean. Remove bread from pan to rack to cool

ZUCCHINI BREAD

Servings: 24 | Prep: 15m | Cooks: 1h10m | Total: 1h25m

NUTRITION FACTS

Calories: 231 | Carbohydrates: 29.6g | Fat: 11.6g | Protein: 2.9g | Cholesterol: 23mg

INGREDIENTS

- 3 eggs
- 3 teaspoons ground cinnamon
- 1 cup vegetable oil
- 1 teaspoon baking soda
- 2 cups white sugar
- 1/4 teaspoon baking powder
- 2 cups grated zucchini
- 1 teaspoon salt
- 2 teaspoons vanilla extract
- 1/2 cup chopped walnuts
- 3 cups all-purpose flour

DIRECTIONS

1. Preheat oven to 325 degrees F (165 degrees C). Grease and flour two 8x4 inch loaf pans.
2. In a large bowl, beat eggs until light and frothy. Mix in oil and sugar. Stir in zucchini and vanilla. Combine flour, cinnamon, soda, baking powder, salt and nuts; stir into the egg mixture. Divide batter into prepared pans.
3. Bake for 60 to 70 minutes, or until done.

TRADITIONAL WHITE BREAD

Servings: 20 | Prep: 20m | Cooks: 30m | Total: 2h30m | Additional: 1h40m

NUTRITION FACTS

INGREDIENTS

- 2 (.25 ounce) packages active dry yeast
- 3 tablespoons lard, softened
- 3 tablespoons white sugar
- 1 tablespoon salt
- 2 1/2 cups warm water (110 degrees F/45 degrees C)
- 6 1/2 cups bread flour

DIRECTIONS

1. In a large bowl, dissolve yeast and sugar in warm water. Stir in lard, salt and two cups of the flour. Stir in the remaining flour, 1/2 cup at a time, beating well after each addition. When the dough has pulled together, turn it out onto a lightly floured surface and knead until smooth and elastic, about 8 minutes.
2. Lightly oil a large bowl, place the dough in the bowl and turn to coat with oil. Cover with a damp cloth and let rise in a warm place until doubled in volume, about 1 hour.
3. Deflate the dough and turn it out onto a lightly floured surface. Divide the dough into two equal pieces and form into loaves. Place the loaves into two lightly greased 9x5 inch loaf pans. Cover the loaves with a damp cloth and let rise until doubled in volume, about 40 minutes.
4. Preheat oven to 425 degrees F (220 degrees C).
5. Bake at 375 degrees F (190 degrees C) for about 30 minutes or until the top is golden brown and the bottom of the loaf sounds hollow when tapped.

CREAMY BANANA BREAD

Servings: 16 | Prep: 30m | Cooks: 45m | Total: 1h15m

NUTRITION FACTS

Calories: 289 | Carbohydrates: 35.5g | Fat: 15.1g | Protein: 4.4g | Cholesterol: 39mg

INGREDIENTS

- 1/2 cup margarine, softened
- 2 1/4 cups all-purpose flour
- 1 (8 ounce) package cream cheese, softened
- 1 1/2 teaspoons baking powder
- 1 1/4 cups white sugar
- 1/2 teaspoon baking soda
- 2 eggs
- 3/4 cup chopped pecans
- 1 cup mashed bananas

- 2 tablespoons brown sugar
- 1 teaspoon vanilla extract
- 2 teaspoons ground cinnamon

DIRECTIONS

1. Preheat oven to 350 degrees F (175 degrees C). Grease and flour two 8x4-inch loaf pans.
2. Cream the margarine and cream cheese together. Gradually add the white sugar, and continue beating until light and fluffy. Add eggs one at a time, beating well after each addition. Stir in the mashed bananas and vanilla. Add flour, baking powder, and baking soda; mix until batter is just moist.
3. In a small bowl, mix together chopped pecans, 2 tablespoons brown sugar, and cinnamon.
4. Divide half the batter between the two prepared loaf pans. Sprinkle pecan mixture over the batter in the pans, and top with remaining batter
5. Bake in the preheated oven until a toothpick inserted in the center of each loaf comes out clean, about 45 minutes.

BEST EVER MUFFINS

Servings: 12 | Prep: 10m | Cooks: 25m | Total: 35m

NUTRITION FACTS

Calories: 181 | Carbohydrates: 29.7g | Fat: 5.6g | Protein: 3.3g | Cholesterol: 17mg

INGREDIENTS

- 2 cups all-purpose flour
- 1 egg
- 3 teaspoons baking powder
- 1 cup milk
- 1/2 teaspoon salt
- 1/4 cup vegetable oil
- 3/4 cup white sugar

DIRECTIONS

1. Preheat oven to 400 degrees F (205 degrees C).
2. Stir together the flour, baking powder, salt and sugar in a large bowl. Make a well in the center. In a small bowl or 2 cup measuring cup, beat egg with a fork. Stir in milk and oil. Pour all at once into

the well in the flour mixture. Mix quickly and lightly with a fork until moistened, but do not beat. The batter will be lumpy. Pour the batter into paper lined muffin pan cups.
3. Variations: Blueberry Muffins: Add 1 cup fresh blueberries. Raisin Muffins: Add 1 cup finely chopped raisins. Date Muffins: Add 1 cup finely chopped dates. Cheese Muffins: Fold in 1 cup grated sharp yellow cheese. Bacon Muffins: Fold 1/4 cup crisp cooked bacon, broken into bits.
4. Bake for 25 minutes, or until golden.

EASY MORNING GLORY MUFFINS
Servings: 12 | Prep: 25m | Cooks: 20m | Total: 45m

NUTRITION FACTS

Calories: 421 | Carbohydrates: 45.3g | Fat: 25.4g | Protein: 5g | Cholesterol: 47mg

INGREDIENTS

- 2 cups all-purpose flour
- 1/2 cup raisins
- 1 1/4 cups white sugar
- 1/2 cup chopped walnuts
- 2 teaspoons baking soda
- 1/2 cup unsweetened flaked coconut
- 2 teaspoons ground cinnamon
- 1 apple - peeled, cored and shredded
- 1/4 teaspoon salt
- 3 eggs
- 2 cups shredded carrots
- 1 cup vegetable oil
- 2 teaspoons vanilla extract

DIRECTIONS

1. Preheat oven to 350 degrees F (175 degrees C). Grease 12 muffin cups, or line with paper muffin liners.
2. In a large bowl, mix together flour, sugar, baking soda, cinnamon, and salt. Stir in the carrot, raisins, nuts, coconut, and apple.
3. In a separate bowl, beat together eggs, oil, and vanilla. Stir egg mixture into the carrot/flour mixture, just until moistened. Scoop batter into prepared muffin cups.

4. Bake in preheated oven for 20 minutes, until a toothpick inserted into center of a muffin comes out clean.

AMAZING WHOLE WHEAT PIZZA CRUST

Servings: 10 | Prep: 25m | Cooks: 20m | Total: 2h45m | Additional: 2h

NUTRITION FACTS

Calories: 167 | Carbohydrates: 32.6g | Fat: 2g | Protein: 5.7g | Cholesterol: 0mg

INGREDIENTS

- 1 teaspoon white sugar
- 1 teaspoon salt
- 1 1/2 cups warm water (110 degrees F/45 degrees C)
- 2 cups whole wheat flour
- 1 tablespoon active dry yeast
- 1 1/2 cups all-purpose flour
- 1 tablespoon olive oil

DIRECTIONS

1. In a large bowl, dissolve sugar in warm water. Sprinkle yeast over the top, and let stand for about 10 minutes, until foamy.
2. Stir the olive oil and salt into the yeast mixture, then mix in the whole wheat flour and 1 cup of the all-purpose flour until dough starts to come together. Tip dough out onto a surface floured with the remaining all-purpose flour, and knead until all of the flour has been absorbed, and the ball of dough becomes smooth, about 10 minutes. Place dough in an oiled bowl, and turn to coat the surface. Cover loosely with a towel, and let stand in a warm place until doubled in size, about 1 hour.
3. When the dough is doubled, tip the dough out onto a lightly floured surface, and divide into 2 pieces for 2 thin crust, or leave whole to make one thick crust. Form into a tight ball. Let rise for about 45 minutes, until doubled.
4. Preheat the oven to 425 degrees F (220 degrees C). Roll a ball of dough with a rolling pin until it will not stretch any further. Then, drape it over both of your fists, and gently pull the edges outward, while rotating the crust. When the circle has reached the desired size, place on a well oiled pizza pan. Top pizza with your favorite toppings, such as sauce, cheese, meats, or vegetables.
5. Bake for 16 to 20 minutes (depending on thickness) in the preheated oven, until the crust is crisp and golden at the edges, and cheese is melted on the top.

BANANA CHOCOLATE CHIP BREAD

Servings: 10 | Prep: 15m | Cooks: 1h10m | Total: 1h25m

Calories: 378 | Carbohydrates: 58.2g | Fat: 15.6g | Protein: 5.1g | Cholesterol: 62mg

INGREDIENTS

- 2 cups all-purpose flour
- 1 teaspoon ground cinnamon, or to taste
- 1 teaspoon baking powder
- 1/2 cup butter, softened
- 1 teaspoon baking soda
- 1 cup white sugar
- 1 teaspoon salt
- 2 eggs
- 3 ripe bananas, mashed
- 1 cup semisweet chocolate chips
- 1 tablespoon milk

DIRECTIONS

1. Preheat oven to 325 degrees F (165 degrees C). Grease a 9x5-inch loaf pan, preferably glass.
2. Mix flour, baking powder, baking soda, and salt in a bowl. Stir bananas, milk, and cinnamon in another bowl. Beat butter and sugar in a third bowl until light and fluffy. Add eggs to butter mixture, one at a time, beating well after each addition. Stir banana mixture into butter mixture. Stir in dry mixture until blended. Fold in chocolate chips until just combined. Pour batter into prepared loaf pan.
3. Bake in the preheated oven until a toothpick inserted into the center comes out clean, about 70 minutes. Cool in the pan for 10 minutes before removing to cool completely on a wire rack before slicing.

LOW-FAT BLUEBERRY BRAN MUFFINS

Servings: 12 | Prep: 15m | Cooks: 20m | Total: 35m

NUTRITION FACTS

Calories: 123 | Carbohydrates: 28.3g | Fat: 0.9g | Protein: 3.7g | Cholesterol: 16mg

INGREDIENTS

- 1 1/2 cups wheat bran
- 1/2 cup all-purpose flour
- 1 cup nonfat milk

* 1/2 cup whole wheat flour
* 1/2 cup unsweetened applesauce
* 1 teaspoon baking soda
* 1 egg
* 1 teaspoon baking powder
* 2/3 cup brown sugar
* 1/2 teaspoon salt
* 1/2 teaspoon vanilla extract
* 1 cup blueberries

DIRECTIONS

1. Preheat oven to 375 degrees F (190 degrees C). Grease muffin cups or use paper muffin liners. Mix together wheat bran and milk, and let stand for 10 minutes.
2. In a large bowl, mix together applesauce, egg, brown sugar, and vanilla. Beat in bran mixture. Sift together all-purpose flour, whole wheat flour, baking soda, baking powder, and salt. Stir into bran mixture until just blended. Fold in blueberries. Scoop into muffin cups.
3. Bake in preheated oven for 15 to 20 minutes, or until tops spring back when lightly tapped.

KENTUCKY BISCUITS

Servings: 12 | Prep: 15m | Cooks: 15m | Total: 30m

NUTRITION FACTS

Calories: 154 | Carbohydrates: 17.9g | Fat: 8g | Protein: 2.7g | Cholesterol: 21mg

INGREDIENTS

* 2 cups all-purpose flour
* 1 tablespoon white sugar
* 2 1/2 teaspoons baking powder
* 1/2 cup butter
* 1/2 teaspoon baking soda
* 3/4 cup buttermilk
* 1 dash salt

DIRECTIONS

1. Preheat oven to 400 degrees F (200 degrees C).
2. In a bowl, mix the flour, baking powder, baking soda, salt, and sugar. Cut in 1/2 cup butter until the mixture resembles coarse crumbs. Mix in the buttermilk. Turn out onto a lightly floured surface, and knead 2 minutes. Transfer to an ungreased baking sheet, roll into a 6x6 inch square, and cut into 12 even sections. Do not separate.
3. Bake 15 minutes in the preheated oven, until a knife inserted in the center of the square comes out clean. Separate into biscuits, and serve hot.

KENTUCKY BISCUITS

Servings: 20 | Prep: 30m | Cooks: 1h | Total: 1h30m

NUTRITION FACTS

Calories: 278 | Carbohydrates: 34.9g | Fat: 15.2g | Protein: 3g | Cholesterol: 28mg

INGREDIENTS

- 2 (1 ounce) squares unsweetened chocolate
- 2 cups all-purpose flour
- 3 eggs
- 1 teaspoon baking soda
- 2 cups white sugar
- 1 teaspoon salt
- 1 cup vegetable oil
- 1 teaspoon ground cinnamon
- 2 cups grated zucchini
- 3/4 cup semisweet chocolate chip
- 1 teaspoon vanilla extract

DIRECTIONS

1. Preheat oven to 350 degrees F (175 degrees C). Lightly grease two 9x5 inch loaf pans. In a microwave-safe bowl, microwave chocolate until melted. Stir occasionally until chocolate is smooth.
2. In a large bowl, combine eggs, sugar, oil, grated zucchini, vanilla and chocolate; beat well. Stir in the flour baking soda, salt and cinnamon. Fold in the chocolate chips. Pour batter into prepared loaf pans.
3. Bake in preheated oven for 60 to 70 minutes, or until a toothpick inserted into the center of a loaf comes out clean.

BASIC BISCUITS

Servings: 10 | Prep: 15m | Cooks: 10m | Total: 25m

NUTRITION FACTS

Calories: 191 | Carbohydrates: 20.2g | Fat: 10.9g | Protein: 3.2g | Cholesterol: 1mg

INGREDIENTS

- 2 cups all-purpose flour
- 1/2 cup shortening
- 1 tablespoon baking powder
- 3/4 cup milk
- 1/2 teaspoon salt

DIRECTIONS

1. Preheat oven to 450 degrees F (230 degrees C).
2. In a large mixing bowl sift together flour, baking powder and salt. Cut in shortening with fork or pastry blender until mixture resembles coarse crumbs.
3. Pour milk into flour mixture while stirring with a fork. Mix in milk until dough is soft, moist and pulls away from the side of the bowl.
4. Turn dough out onto a lightly floured surface and toss with flour until no longer sticky. Roll dough out into a 1/2 inch thick sheet and cut with a floured biscuit or cookie cutter. Press together unused dough and repeat rolling and cutting procedure.
5. Place biscuits on ungreased baking sheets and bake in preheated oven until golden brown, about 10 minutes.

BURGER OR HOT DOG BUNS

Servings: 12 | Prep: 20m | Cooks: 10m | Total: 1h30m | Additional: 1h

NUTRITION FACTS

Calories: 230 | Carbohydrates: 39.1g | Fat: 5.1g | Protein: 6.3g | Cholesterol: 27mg

INGREDIENTS

- 1 cup milk
- 1 (.25 ounce) package instant yeast
- 1/2 cup water
- 2 tablespoons white sugar
- 1/4 cup butter

- 1 1/2 teaspoons salt
- 4 1/2 cups all-purpose flour
- 1 egg

DIRECTIONS

1. In a small saucepan, heat milk, water and butter until very warm, 120 degrees F (50 degrees C).
2. In a large bowl, mix together 1 3/4 cup flour, yeast, sugar and salt. Mix milk mixture into flour mixture, and then mix in egg. Stir in the remaining flour, 1/2 cup at a time, beating well after each addition. When the dough has pulled together, turn it out onto a lightly floured surface, and knead until smooth and elastic, about 8 minutes.
3. Divide dough into 12 equal pieces. Shape into smooth balls, and place on a greased baking sheet. Flatten slightly. Cover, and let rise for 30 to 35 minutes.
4. Bake at 400 degrees F (200 degrees C) for 10 to 12 minutes, or until golden brown.
5. For Hot Dog Buns: Shape each piece into a 6x4 inch rectangle. Starting with the longer side, roll up tightly, and pinch edges and ends to seal. Let rise about 20 to 25 minutes. Bake as above. These buns are pretty big. I usually make 16 instead of 12.

MORNING GLORY MUFFINS
Servings: 18 | Prep: 15m | Cooks: 20m | Total: 35m

NUTRITION FACTS

Calories: 194 | Carbohydrates: 37.3g | Fat: 4.2g | Protein: 3.1g | Cholesterol: 10mg

INGREDIENTS

- 1 1/2 cups all-purpose flour
- 1 apple - peeled, cored, and chopped
- 1/2 cup whole wheat flour
- 1 cup raisins
- 1 1/4 cups white sugar
- 1 egg
- 1 tablespoon ground cinnamon
- 2 egg whites
- 2 teaspoons baking powder
- 1/2 cup apple butter
- 1/2 teaspoon baking soda
- 1/4 cup vegetable oil
- 1/2 teaspoon salt
- 1 tablespoon vanilla extract

- 2 cups grated carrots
- 2 tablespoons chopped walnuts
- 2 tablespoons toasted wheat germ

DIRECTIONS

1. Preheat oven to 375 degrees F (190 degrees C). Lightly oil 18 muffin cups, or coat with nonstick cooking spray.
2. In a medium bowl, whisk together eggs, egg whites, apple butter, oil and vanilla.
3. In a large bowl, stir together flours, sugar, cinnamon, baking powder, baking soda and salt. Stir in carrots, apples and raisins. Stir in apple butter mixture until just moistened. Spoon the batter into the prepared muffin cups, filling them about 3/4 full.
4. In a small bowl, combine walnuts and wheat germ; sprinkle over the muffin tops.
5. Bake at 375 degrees F (190 degrees C) for 15 to 20 minutes, or until the tops are golden and spring back when lightly pressed.

LEMON BLUEBERRY BREAD

Servings: 12 | Prep: 30m | Cooks: 1h | Total: 1h30m

NUTRITION FACTS

Calories: 241 | Carbohydrates: 36.5g | Fat: 9.5g | Protein: 3.9g | Cholesterol: 45mg

INGREDIENTS

- 1/3 cup melted butter
- 1/2 cup milk
- 1 cup white sugar
- 2 tablespoons grated lemon zest
- 3 tablespoons lemon juice
- 1/2 cup chopped walnuts
- 2 eggs
- 1 cup fresh or frozen blueberries
- 1 1/2 cups all-purpose flour
- 2 tablespoons lemon juice
- 1 teaspoon baking powder
- 1/4 cup white sugar
- 1 teaspoon salt

DIRECTIONS

1. Preheat oven to 350 degrees F (175 degrees C). Lightly grease an 8x4 inch loaf pan.
2. In a mixing bowl, beat together butter, 1 cup sugar, juice and eggs. Combine flour, baking powder and salt; stir into egg mixture alternately with milk. Fold in lemon zest, nuts, and blueberries. Pour batter into prepared pan.
3. Bake in preheated oven for 60 to 70 minutes, until a toothpick inserted into center of the loaf comes out clean. Cool bread in pan for 10 minutes. Meanwhile, combine lemon juice and 1/4 cup sugar in a small bowl. Remove bread from pan and drizzle with glaze. Cool on a wire rack.

SARAH'S BANANA BREAD MUFFINS
Servings: 12 | Prep: 10m | Cooks: 35m | Total: 45m

NUTRITION FACTS

Calories: 270 | Carbohydrates: 39.7g | Fat: 11.5g | Protein: 3.4g | Cholesterol: 16mg

INGREDIENTS

- 1 cup white sugar
- 1/4 cup chopped walnuts
- 1/2 cup vegetable oil
- 2 cups all-purpose flour
- 1 egg
- 1 teaspoon baking soda
- 3 ripe bananas, mashed
- 1/2 teaspoon salt

DIRECTIONS

1. Preheat oven to 350 degrees F (175 degrees C). Place muffin cups in muffin tin, or grease with a little butter.
2. Mix sugar, oil, and egg until creamy and light yellow in a bowl. Add bananas and walnuts. Add flour, baking soda, and salt. Stir until completely smooth. Spoon the batter into the muffin tin.
3. Bake for 30 to 40 minutes, until toothpick poked in center muffin comes out clean.

SOPHIE'S ZUCCHINI BREAD
Servings: 24 | Prep: 10m | Cooks: 1h | Total: 1h10m

Calories: 248 | Carbohydrates: 30.1g | Fat: 13.1g | Protein: 3.3g | Cholesterol: 23mg

INGREDIENTS

- 3 cups all-purpose flour
- 2 cups white sugar
- 1 teaspoon salt
- 3 teaspoons vanilla extract
- 1 teaspoon baking soda
- 1 cup vegetable oil
- 3 teaspoons ground cinnamon
- 3 cups grated zucchini
- 1/4 teaspoon baking powder
- 1 cup chopped walnuts (optional)
- 3 eggs

DIRECTIONS

1. Preheat oven to 350 degrees F (175 degrees C).
2. Sift together flour, salt, soda, cinnamon, baking powder.
3. Beat eggs. Add and mix well sugar, vanilla, and oil. Add zucchini to egg mixture. Add dry ingredients, mixing well. Stir in nuts if desired. Pour into 2 ungreased loaf pans.
4. Bake at 350 degrees F (175 degrees C) for 1 hour.

CRANBERRY ORANGE LOAF

Servings: 12 | Prep: 15m | Cooks: 1h | Total: 1h25m | Additional: 10m

NUTRITION FACTS

Calories: 224 | Carbohydrates: 36.6g | Fat: 7.7g | Protein: 3.3g | Cholesterol: 16mg

INGREDIENTS

- 2 cups all-purpose flour
- 1/2 cup pecans, coarsely chopped
- 1 1/2 teaspoons baking powder
- 1/4 cup margarine, softened
- 1/2 teaspoon baking soda
- 1 cup white sugar

- 1/2 teaspoon salt
- 1 egg
- 1 tablespoon grated orange zest
- 3/4 cup orange juice
- 1 1/2 cups fresh cranberries

DIRECTIONS

1. Preheat the oven to 350 degrees F (175 degrees C). Grease and flour a 9x5 inch loaf pan. Whisk together flour, baking powder, baking soda, and salt. Stir in orange zest, cranberries, and pecans. Set aside.
2. In a large bowl, cream together margarine, sugar, and egg until smooth. Stir in orange juice. Beat in flour mixture until just moistened. Pour into prepared pan.
3. Bake for 1 hour in the preheated oven, or until the bread springs back when lightly touched. Let stand 10 minutes, then turn out onto a wire rack to cool. Wrap in plastic when completely cool.

UNBELIEVABLE ROLLS

Servings: 16 | Prep: 30m | Cooks: 15m | Total: 2h15m | Additional: 1h30m

NUTRITION FACTS

Calories: 235 | Carbohydrates: 37.2g | Fat: 6.9g | Protein: 5.7g | Cholesterol: 24mg

INGREDIENTS

- 3/4 cup milk
- 2 eggs
- 3/4 cup water
- 5 teaspoons active dry yeast
- 1/2 cup white sugar
- 5 cups all-purpose flour
- 1 teaspoon salt
- 1/2 cup margarine, melted

DIRECTIONS

1. In a medium saucepan over medium heat, warm milk, water, sugar and salt. Remove from heat, and mix in the eggs and yeast.
2. Measure flour into a large bowl. Make a well in the flour, and pour milk mixture into it. Do not stir. Cover with a lid, and let stand for 20 to 30 minutes.

3. Pour melted margarine into flour, and mix well. Add more flour if too sticky. Knead lightly. Cover, and let rise for 20 to 30 minutes.

4. Shape the dough into rolls, and place on a baking sheet. Let rise again for 20 to 30 minutes.

5. Bake rolls in a preheated 400 degrees F (205 degrees C) oven for 15 minutes, or until done.

WHOLE WHEAT HONEY BREAD

Servings: 12 | Prep: 5m | Cooks: 3h | Total: 3h5m

NUTRITION FACTS

Calories: 148 | Carbohydrates: 30g | Fat: 2.2g | Protein: 4.6g | Cholesterol: 0mg

INGREDIENTS

- 1 1/8 cups water
- 1 tablespoon dry milk powder
- 3 cups whole wheat flour
- 1 1/2 tablespoons shortening
- 1 1/2 teaspoons salt
- 1 1/2 teaspoons active dry yeast
- 1/3 cup honey

DIRECTIONS

1. Place ingredients in bread machine pan in the order suggested by the manufacturer. Select Whole Wheat setting, and then press Start.

BEST OF THE BEST BLUEBERRY MUFFINS

Servings: 12 | Prep: 15m | Cooks: 30m | Total: 45m

NUTRITION FACTS

Calories: 264 | Carbohydrates: 43.5g | Fat: 8.9g | Protein: 3.8g | Cholesterol: 52mg

INGREDIENTS

- 1/2 cup unsalted butter
- 2 teaspoons baking powder
- 1 1/4 cups white sugar
- 1/2 cup buttermilk
- 1/2 teaspoon salt

- 1 pint fresh blueberries - rinsed, drained and patted dry
- 2 eggs
- 2 tablespoons white sugar
- 2 cups all-purpose flour, divided

DIRECTIONS

1. Position rack in the middle of oven. Preheat oven to 375 degrees F (190 degrees C). Spray the top of a muffin pan with non-stick coating, and line with paper liners.
2. In a large bowl, cream together the butter, 1 1/4 cups sugar and salt until light and fluffy. Beat in the eggs one at a time. Mix together 1 3/4 cup of the flour and baking powder. Beat in the flour mixture alternately with the buttermilk, mixing just until incorporated. Crush 1/4 of the blueberries, and stir into the batter. Mix the rest of the whole blueberries with the remaining 1/4 cup of the flour, and fold into the batter. Scoop into muffin cups. Sprinkle tops lightly with sugar.
3. Bake in preheated oven for 30 minutes, or until golden brown, and tops spring back when lightly tapped.

ALMOST NO FAT BANANA BREAD
Servings: 12 | Prep: 10m | Cooks: 55m | Total: 1h5m

NUTRITION FACTS

Calories: 127 | Carbohydrates: 29.5g | Fat: 0.2g | Protein: 2.4g | Cholesterol: 0mg

INGREDIENTS

- 1 1/2 cups all-purpose flour
- 1/2 teaspoon ground cinnamon
- 3/4 cup white sugar
- 2 egg whites
- 1 1/4 teaspoons baking powder
- 1 cup banana, mashed
- 1/2 teaspoon baking soda
- 1/4 cup applesauce

DIRECTIONS

1. Preheat oven to 350 degrees F (175 degrees C). Lightly grease an 8x4 inch loaf pan.
2. In a large bowl, stir together flour, sugar, baking powder, baking soda and cinnamon. Add egg whites, bananas and applesauce; stir just until combined. Pour batter into prepared pan.

3. Bake in preheated oven for 50 to 55 minutes, until a toothpick inserted into center of loaf comes out clean. Turn out onto wire rack and allow to cool before slicing.

ZUCCHINI-CHOCOLATE CHIP MUFFINS

Servings: 12 | Prep: 15m | Cooks: 20m | Total: 50m | Additional: 15m

NUTRITION FACTS

Calories: 265 | Carbohydrates: 30.6g | Fat: 15.2g | Protein: 3.5g | Cholesterol: 16mg

INGREDIENTS

- 1 1/2 cups all-purpose flour
- 1/4 cup milk
- 3/4 cup white sugar
- 1 tablespoon lemon juice
- 1 teaspoon baking soda
- 1 teaspoon vanilla extract
- 1 teaspoon ground cinnamon
- 1 cup shredded zucchini
- 1/2 teaspoon salt
- 1/2 cup miniature semisweet chocolate chips
- 1 egg, lightly beaten
- 1/2 cup chopped walnuts
- 1/2 cup vegetable oil

DIRECTIONS

1. Preheat oven to 350 degrees F (175 degrees C). Grease 12 muffin cups, or line with paper muffin liners.
2. Combine flour, sugar, baking soda, cinnamon, and salt in a large bowl. Mix egg, oil, milk, lemon juice, and vanilla extract in a bowl; stir into dry ingredients until just moistened. Fold in zucchini, chocolate chips, and walnuts. Fill prepared muffin cups 2/3 full.
3. Bake in preheated oven until a toothpick inserted into the center of a muffin comes out clean, 20 to 25 minutes.

PEPPY'S PITA BREAD

Servings: 8 | Prep: 30m | Cooks: 15m | Total: 3h20m | Additional: 2h35m

NUTRITION FACTS

Calories: 191 | Carbohydrates: 36.8g | Fat: 2.2g | Protein: 5.1g | Cholesterol: 0mg

INGREDIENTS

- 1 1/8 cups warm water (110 degrees F/45 degrees C)
- 1 tablespoon vegetable oil
- 3 cups all-purpose flour
- 1 1/2 teaspoons white sugar
- 1 teaspoon salt
- 1 1/2 teaspoons active dry yeast

DIRECTIONS

1. Place all ingredients in bread pan of your bread machine, select Dough setting and start. When dough has risen long enough, machine will beep.
2. Turn dough onto a lightly floured surface. Gently roll and stretch dough into a 12 inch rope. With a sharp knife, divide dough into 8 pieces. Roll each into a smooth ball. With a rolling pin, roll each ball into a 6 to 7 inch circle. Set aside on a lightly floured countertop. cover with a towel. Let pitas rise about 30 minutes until slightly puffy.
3. Preheat oven to 500 degrees F (260 degrees C). Place 2 or 3 pitas on a wire cake rack. Place cake rack directly on oven rack. Bake pitas 4 to 5 minutes until puffed and tops begin to brown. Remove from oven and immediately place pitas in a sealed brown paper bag or cover them with a damp kitchen towel until soft. Once pitas a softened, either cut in half or split top edge for half or whole pitas. They can be stored in a plastic bag in the refrigerator for several days or in the freezer for 1 or 2 months.

CHOCOLATE CHIP BANANA BREAD

Servings: 20 | Prep: 15m | Cooks: 1h15m | Total: 1h30m

NUTRITION FACTS

Calories: 346 | Carbohydrates: 48.4g | Fat: 16.5g | Protein: 4g | Cholesterol: 19mg

INGREDIENTS

- 1 cup shortening
- 1/2 teaspoon salt
- 2 cups white sugar
- 1 teaspoon baking powder
- 2 eggs
- 2 teaspoons baking soda
- 2 tablespoons mayonnaise

- 1 cup semi-sweet chocolate chips
- 6 very ripe bananas, mashed
- 1/2 cup chopped walnuts
- 3 cups all-purpose flour

DIRECTIONS

1. Preheat oven to 350 degrees F (175 degrees C). Lightly grease two 9x5 inch loaf pans.
2. In a large bowl, cream together the shortening and sugar until light and fluffy. Stir in the eggs one at a time, beating well with each addition. Stir in the mayonnaise and bananas. Stir together the flour, salt, baking powder and baking soda. Blend the flour mixture into the banana mixture; stir just enough to evenly combine. Fold in the chocolate chips and walnuts.
3. Bake at 350 degrees F (175 degrees C) until a toothpick inserted into the center of the loaf comes out clean, about 50 to 75 minutes. Cool loaf in the pan for 20 minutes before removing to a wire rack to cool completely.

HEALTH NUT BLUEBERRY MUFFINS

Servings: 12 | Prep: 15m | Cooks: 15m | Total: 30m

NUTRITION FACTS

Calories: 196 | Carbohydrates: 33.4g | Fat: 5.8g | Protein: 5.1g | Cholesterol: 16mg

INGREDIENTS

- 3/4 cup all-purpose flour
- 1/4 teaspoon salt
- 3/4 cup whole wheat flour
- 1 cup blueberries
- 3/4 cup white sugar
- 1/2 cup chopped walnuts
- 1/4 cup oat bran
- 1 banana, mashed
- 1/4 cup quick cooking oats
- 1 cup buttermilk
- 1/4 cup wheat germ
- 1 egg
- 1 teaspoon baking powder
- 1 tablespoon vegetable oil
- 1 teaspoon baking soda

- 1 teaspoon vanilla extract

DIRECTIONS

1. Preheat the oven to 350 degrees F (175 degrees C). Grease a 12 cup muffin pan, or line with paper muffin cups.
2. In a large bowl, stir together the all-purpose flour, whole wheat flour, sugar, oat bran, quick-cooking oats, wheat germ, baking powder, baking soda and salt. Gently stir in the blueberries and walnuts. In a separate bowl, mix together the mashed banana, buttermilk, egg, oil and vanilla. Pour the wet ingredients into the dry, and mix just until blended. Spoon into muffin cups, filling all the way to the top.
3. Bake for 15 to 18 minutes in the preheated oven, or until the tops of the muffins spring back when lightly touched.

LIGHT OAT BREAD

Servings: 12 | Prep: 5m | Cooks: 3h | Total: 3h5m

NUTRITION FACTS

Calories: 152 | Carbohydrates: 28.6g | Fat: 2.3g | Protein: 3.9g | Cholesterol: 0mg

INGREDIENTS

- 1 1/4 cups water
- 1/2 cup rolled oats
- 2 tablespoons margarine
- 2 tablespoons brown sugar
- 1 teaspoon salt
- 1 1/2 teaspoons active dry yeast
- 3 cups all-purpose flour

DIRECTIONS

1. Add ingredients to bread machine pan in order recommended by your manufacturer. Use regular light setting.

WHITE BREAD FOR THE BREAD MACHINE

Servings: 12 | Prep: 5m | Cooks: 3h | Total: 3h5m

NUTRITION FACTS

Calories: 168 | Carbohydrates: 28.3g | Fat: 4g | Protein: 4.4g | Cholesterol: 0mg

INGREDIENTS

- 1 cup warm water (110 degrees F/45 degrees C)
- 3 tablespoons vegetable oil
- 3 tablespoons white sugar
- 3 cups bread flour
- 1 1/2 teaspoons salt
- 2 1/4 teaspoons active dry yeast

DIRECTIONS

1. Place water, sugar, salt, oil, bread flour and yeast into pan of bread machine.
2. Bake on White Bread setting. Cool on wire racks before slicing.

BREAD MACHINE BAGELS

Servings: 9 | Prep: 30m | Cooks: 3h25m | Total: 3h55m

NUTRITION FACTS

Calories: 50 | Carbohydrates: 8.8g | Fat: 1.3g | Protein: 1.4g | Cholesterol: 0mg

INGREDIENTS

- 1 cup warm water (110 degrees F/45 degrees C)
- 3 quarts boiling water
- 1 1/2 teaspoons salt
- 3 tablespoons white sugar
- 2 tablespoons white sugar
- 1 tablespoon cornmeal
- 3 cups bread flour
- 1 egg white
- 2 1/4 teaspoons active dry yeast
- 3 tablespoons poppy seeds

DIRECTIONS

1. Place water, salt, sugar, flour and yeast in the bread machine pan in the order recommended by the manufacturer. Select Dough setting.
2. When cycle is complete, let dough rest on a lightly floured surface. Meanwhile, in a large pot bring 3 quarts of water to a boil. Stir in 3 tablespoons of sugar.
3. Cut dough into 9 equal pieces, and roll each piece into a small ball. Flatten balls. Poke a hole in the middle of each with your thumb. Twirl the dough on your finger or thumb to enlarge the hole, and to even out the dough around the hole. Cover bagels with a clean cloth, and let rest for 10 minutes.
4. Sprinkle an ungreased baking sheet with cornmeal. Carefully transfer bagels to boiling water. Boil for 1 minute, turning half way through. Drain briefly on clean towel. Arrange boiled bagels on baking sheet. Glaze tops with egg white, and sprinkle with your choice of toppings.
5. Bake in a preheated 375 degree F (190 degrees C) oven for 20 to 25 minutes, until well browned.

APPLE PIE MUFFINS

Servings: 12 | Prep: 15m | Cooks: 25m | Total: 40m

NUTRITION FACTS

Calories: 312 | Carbohydrates: 51.1g | Fat: 10.5g | Protein: 4.2g | Cholesterol: 42mg

INGREDIENTS

- 2 1/4 cups all-purpose flour
- 1 1/2 cups packed brown sugar
- 1 teaspoon baking soda
- 2 cups diced apples
- 1/2 teaspoon salt
- 1/2 cup packed brown sugar
- 1 egg
- 1/3 cup all-purpose flour
- 1 cup buttermilk
- 1 teaspoon ground cinnamon
- 1/2 cup butter, melted
- 2 tablespoons butter, melted
- 1 teaspoon vanilla extract

DIRECTIONS

1. Preheat the oven to 375 degrees F (190 degrees C). Grease a 12 cup muffin tin or line with paper muffin cups.

2. In a large bowl, stir together 2 1/4 cups flour, baking soda and salt. In a separate smaller bowl, mix together the egg, buttermilk, 1/2 cup melted butter, vanilla and 1 1/2 cups of brown sugar until sugar has dissolved. Pour into the flour mixture and sprinkle the diced apple into the bowl as well. Stir just until everything is blended. Spoon into the prepared muffin tin, filling the cups to the top.
3. In a small bowl, stir together 1/2 cup of brown sugar, 1/3 cup flour and cinnamon. Drizzle in 2 tablespoons of melted butter while tossing with a fork until well blended. Sprinkle this over the tops of the muffins.
4. Bake for 25 minutes in the preheated oven, or until the tops of the muffins spring back when lightly pressed.

CHOCOLATE CHIP PUMPKIN BREAD

Servings: 36 | Prep: 30m | Cooks: 1h | Total: 1h30m

NUTRITION FACTS

Calories: 210 | Carbohydrates: 30.5g | Fat: 9.4g | Protein: 2.6g | Cholesterol: 21mg

INGREDIENTS

- 3 cups white sugar
- 1 tablespoon ground cinnamon
- 1 (15 ounce) can pumpkin puree
- 1 tablespoon ground nutmeg
- 1 cup vegetable oil
- 2 teaspoons baking soda
- 2/3 cup water
- 1 1/2 teaspoons salt
- 4 eggs
- 1 cup miniature semisweet chocolate chips
- 3 1/2 cups all-purpose flour
- 1/2 cup chopped walnuts (optional)

DIRECTIONS

1. Preheat oven to 350 degrees F (175 degrees C). Grease and flour three 1 pound size coffee cans, or three 9x5 inch loaf pans.
2. In a large bowl, combine sugar, pumpkin, oil, water, and eggs. Beat until smooth. Blend in flour, cinnamon, nutmeg, baking soda, and salt. Fold in chocolate chips and nuts. Fill cans 1/2 to 3/4 full.
3. Bake for 1 hour, or until an inserted knife comes out clean. Cool on wire racks before removing from cans or pans.

EASY PUMPKIN MUFFINS

Servings: 12 | Prep: 5m | Cooks: 25m | Total: 30m

NUTRITION FACTS

Calories: 199 | Carbohydrates: 36.8g | Fat: 5.2g | Protein: 2.3g | Cholesterol: 1mg

INGREDIENTS

- 1 (18.25 ounce) package yellow cake mix
- 1/2 teaspoon ground nutmeg
- 1 (15 ounce) can pumpkin puree
- 1/4 teaspoon ground cloves
- 1 teaspoon ground cinnamon

DIRECTIONS

1. Preheat the oven to 350 degrees F (175 degrees C). Grease a 12 cup muffin pan or line with paper liners.
2. In a large bowl, mix together the cake mix, pumpkin puree, cinnamon, nutmeg and cloves until smooth. Spoon equal amounts of batter into the prepared muffin cups.
3. Bake for 20 to 25 minutes in the preheated oven, until a toothpick inserted in the center of one comes out clean.

CINNAMON RAISIN BREAD

Servings: 36 | Prep: 30m | Cooks: 45m | Total: 3h20m | Additional: 2h5m

NUTRITION FACTS

Calories: 182 | Carbohydrates: 32.4g | Fat: 4.1g | Protein: 4.1g | Cholesterol: 18mg

INGREDIENTS

- 1 1/2 cups milk
- 1 cup raisins
- 1 cup warm water (110 degrees F/45 degrees C)
- 8 cups all-purpose flour
- 2 (.25 ounce) packages active dry yeast
- 2 tablespoons milk

- 3 eggs
- 3/4 cup white sugar
- 1/2 cup white sugar
- 2 tablespoons ground cinnamon
- 1 teaspoon salt
- 2 tablespoons butter, melted
- 1/2 cup margarine, softened

DIRECTIONS

1. Warm the milk in a small saucepan until it bubbles, then remove from heat. Let cool until lukewarm.
2. Dissolve yeast in warm water, and set aside until yeast is frothy. Mix in eggs, sugar, butter or margarine, salt, and raisins. Stir in cooled milk. Add the flour gradually to make a stiff dough.
3. Knead dough on a lightly floured surface for a few minutes. Place in a large, greased, mixing bowl, and turn to grease the surface of the dough. Cover with a damp cloth. Allow to rise until doubled.
4. Roll out on a lightly floured surface into a large rectangle 1/2 inch thick. Moisten dough with 2 tablespoons milk. Mix together 3/4 cup sugar and 2 tablespoons cinnamon, and sprinkle mixture on top of the moistened dough. Roll up tightly; the roll should be about 3 inches in diameter. Cut into thirds, and tuck under ends. Place loaves into well greased 9 x 5 inch pans. Lightly grease tops of loaves. Let rise again for 1 hour.
5. Bake at 350 degrees F (175 degrees C) for 45 minutes, or until loaves are lightly browned and sound hollow when knocked. Remove loaves from pans, and brush with melted butter or margarine. Let cool before slicing.

BASIC CORN MUFFINS

Servings: 12 | Prep: 10m | Cooks: 20m | Total: 30m

NUTRITION FACTS

Calories: 154 | Carbohydrates: 22.5g | Fat: 5.9g | Protein: 3.1g | Cholesterol: 17mg

INGREDIENTS

- 1 cup cornmeal
- 1/2 teaspoon salt
- 1 cup all-purpose flour
- 1 egg, beaten
- 1/3 cup white sugar
- 1/4 cup canola oil

- 2 teaspoons baking powder
- 1 cup milk

DIRECTIONS

1. Preheat oven to 400 degrees F (200 degrees C). Grease muffin pan or line with paper muffin liners.
2. In a large bowl, mix together corn meal, flour, sugar, baking powder and salt. Add egg, oil and milk; stir gently to combine. Spoon batter into prepared muffin cups.
3. Bake at 400 degrees F (200 degrees C) for 15 to 20 minutes, or until a toothpick inserted into a muffin comes out clean.

CHEF JOHN'S BANANA BREAD

Servings: 12 | Prep: 15m | Cooks: 1h10m | Total: 1h45m | Additional: 20m

NUTRITION FACTS

Calories: 334 | Carbohydrates: 43.8g | Fat: 16.6g | Protein: 5.3g | Cholesterol: 51mg

INGREDIENTS

- cooking spray
- 1 cup white sugar
- 2 cups all-purpose flour
- 2 large eggs
- 1 teaspoon salt
- 1/4 teaspoon vanilla extract
- 1 teaspoon baking powder
- 1 tablespoon milk
- 1 teaspoon baking soda
- 1 cup chopped walnuts
- 1/2 cup butter, softened
- 1/3 cup semisweet chocolate chips
- 3 ripe bananas, mashed

DIRECTIONS

1. Preheat the oven to 325 degrees F (165 degrees C). Coat a 9x4-inch loaf pan with cooking spray.
2. Whisk flour, salt, baking powder, and baking soda together in a bowl.

3. Beat butter and sugar with an electric mixer in a large bowl until smooth. Add mashed bananas and beat until combined. Beat eggs into the butter mixture one at a time, fully blending each egg before adding the next. Stir vanilla extract and milk into the mixture.
4. Stir chopped walnuts, chocolate chips, and flour mixture into banana mixture until just incorporated.
5. Pour batter into the prepared loaf pan. Tap pan on the counter to release any air pockets.
6. Bake in preheated oven for about 1 hour 10 minutes, or until an inserted toothpick comes out clean.
7. Let the bread rest in the pan for 15-20 minutes; remove from pan, slice, and serve.

SWEET CORNBREAD CAKE

Servings: 12 | Prep: 10m | Cooks: 45m | Total: 55m

NUTRITION FACTS

Calories: 461 | Carbohydrates: 61.1g | Fat: 21g | Protein: 7.9g | Cholesterol: 81mg

INGREDIENTS

- 1 cup cornmeal
- 2/3 cup vegetable oil
- 3 cups all-purpose flour
- 1/3 cup melted butter
- 1 1/3 cups white sugar
- 2 tablespoons honey
- 2 tablespoons baking powder
- 4 eggs, beaten
- 1 teaspoon salt
- 2 1/2 cups whole milk

DIRECTIONS

1. Preheat oven to 350 degrees F (175 degrees C), and grease a 9x13 inch baking dish.
2. Stir together the cornmeal, flour, sugar, baking powder, and salt in a mixing bowl. Pour in the vegetable oil, melted butter, honey, beaten eggs, and milk, and stir just to moisten.
3. Pour the batter into the prepared baking dish and bake in the preheated oven for 45 minutes, until the top of the cornbread starts to brown and show cracks.

IRISH SODA BREAD

Servings: 8 | Prep: 15m | Cooks: 1h5m | Total: 1h25m | Additional: 5m

NUTRITION FACTS

Calories: 511 | Carbohydrates: 99.5g | Fat: 8.6g | Protein: 11.3g | Cholesterol: 11.3mg

INGREDIENTS

- 1/2 cup white sugar
- 3 cups raisins
- 4 cups all-purpose flour
- 1 tablespoon caraway seeds
- 2 teaspoons baking powder
- 2 eggs, lightly beaten
- 1 teaspoon baking soda
- 1 1/4 cups buttermilk
- 3/4 teaspoon salt
- 1 cup sour cream

DIRECTIONS

1. Preheat oven to 350 degrees F (175 degrees C). Grease a 9 inch round cast iron skillet or a 9 inch round baking or cake pan.
2. In a mixing bowl, combine flour (reserving 1 tablespoon), sugar, baking powder, baking soda, salt, raisins and caraway seeds. In a small bowl, blend eggs, buttermilk and sour cream. Stir the liquid mixture into flour mixture just until flour is moistened. Knead dough in bowl about 10 to 12 strokes. Dough will be sticky. Place the dough in the prepared skillet or pan and pat down. Cut a 4x3/4 inch deep slit in the top of the bread. Dust with reserved flour
3. Bake in a preheated 350 degrees F (175 degrees C) oven for 65 to 75 minutes. Let cool and turn bread onto a wire rack.

STREUSEL TOPPED BLUEBERRY MUFFINS

Servings: 12 | Prep: 20m | Cooks: 25m | Total: 45m

NUTRITION FACTS

Calories: 266 | Carbohydrates: 38.9g | Fat: 10.9g | Protein: 4g | Cholesterol: 57mg

INGREDIENTS

- 2 cups all-purpose flour
- 1 teaspoon vanilla extract
- 2 teaspoons baking powder
- 1/4 teaspoon lemon zest
- 1/2 teaspoon salt
- 1/2 cup milk

- 1 1/2 tablespoons all-purpose flour
- 2 tablespoons all-purpose flour
- 1 1/2 cups fresh blueberries
- 5 tablespoons white sugar
- 1/2 cup butter
- 1/2 teaspoon ground cinnamon
- 3/4 cup white sugar
- 2 tablespoons butter, diced
- 2 eggs

DIRECTIONS

1. Preheat oven to 375 degrees F (190 degrees C). Grease 12 muffin cups or line with paper muffin liners.
2. Combine 2 cups flour, 2 teaspoons baking powder, and 1/2 teaspoon salt in medium bowl. In a small bowl, sprinkle 1 to 2 tablespoons flour over blueberries, and set aside. (This simple trick will keep you from having "purple" batter)
3. In a large bowl, beat 1/2 cup butter with 3/4 cup sugar until light and fluffy. Beat in eggs, and stir in vanilla and lemon zest. Fold in dry ingredients alternately with milk. Fold in blueberries. Remember, fold gently, don't stir. Spoon batter into prepared cups.
4. Combine 2 tablespoons flour, 5 tablespoons sugar ,and 1/2 teaspoon cinnamon in a small bowl. Cut in 2 tablespoons butter with fork or pastry blender until mixture resembles course crumbs. Sprinkle over batter in muffin cups.
5. Bake in the preheated oven for 20 to 25 minutes, or until a toothpick inserted in center of a muffin comes out clean. Cool in pans on wire rack. These muffins freeze really well, and re-heat in the microwave successfully. Hope you enjoy.

CINNAMON SWIRL BREAD

Servings: 12 | Prep: 10m | Cooks: 45m | Total: 1h | Additional: 5m

NUTRITION FACTS

Calories: 233 | Carbohydrates: 39.6g | Fat: 7.1g | Protein: 3.4g | Cholesterol: 17mg

INGREDIENTS

- 1/3 cup white sugar
- 1 cup white sugar
- 2 teaspoons ground cinnamon
- 1 egg, beaten
- 2 cups all-purpose flour

- 1 cup milk
- 1 tablespoon baking powder
- 1/3 cup vegetable oil
- 1/2 teaspoon salt

DIRECTIONS

1. Preheat oven to 350 degrees F (175 degrees C). Lightly grease a 9x5 inch loaf pan. In a small bowl, mix together 1/3 cup sugar and 2 teaspoons cinnamon; set aside.
2. In large bowl combine flour, baking powder, salt and remaining 1 cup sugar. Combine egg, milk, and oil; add to flour mixture. Stir until just moistened.
3. Pour half of the batter into pan. Sprinkle with half the reserved cinnamon/sugar mixture. Repeat with remaining batter and cinnamon/sugar mixture. Draw a knife through batter to marble.
4. Bake in preheated oven for 45 to 50 minutes, or until a toothpick inserted into center of the loaf comes out clean. Let cool in pan for 10 minutes before removing to a wire rack to cool completely. Wrap in foil and let sit overnight before slicing.

WORLD'S BEST SCONES! FROM SCOTLAND TO THE SAVOY TO THE U.S.

Servings: 8 | Prep: 20m | Cooks: 15m | Total: 35m

NUTRITION FACTS

Calories: 247 | Carbohydrates: 35.4g | Fat: 10g | Protein: 4.8g | Cholesterol: 47mg

INGREDIENTS

- 1 3/4 cups all-purpose flour
- 1/2 cup dried currants or raisins
- 4 teaspoons baking powder
- 1/2 cup milk
- 1/4 cup white sugar
- 1/4 cup sour cream
- 1/8 teaspoon salt
- 1 egg
- 5 tablespoons unsalted butter
- 1 tablespoon milk

DIRECTIONS

1. Preheat the oven to 400 degrees F (200 degrees C).
2. Sift the flour, baking powder, sugar and salt into a large bowl. Cut in butter using a pastry blender or rubbing between your fingers until it is in pea sized lumps. Stir in the currants. Mix together 1/2 cup milk and sour cream in a measuring cup. Pour all at once into the dry ingredients, and stir gently until well blended. Overworking the dough results in terrible scones!
3. With floured hands, pat scone dough into balls 2 to 3 inches across, depending on what size you want. Place onto a greased baking sheet, and flatten lightly. Let the scones barely touch each other. Whisk together the egg and 1 tablespoon of milk. Brush the tops of the scones with the egg wash. Let them rest for about 10 minutes.
4. Bake for 10 to 15 minutes in the preheated oven, until the tops are golden brown, not deep brown. Break each scone apart, or slice in half. Serve with butter or clotted cream and a selection of jams - or even plain.

CHALLAH

Servings: 30 | Prep: 30m | Cooks:40m | Total: 3h40m | Additional: 2h30m

NUTRITION FACTS

Calories: 165 | Carbohydrates: 30.3g | Fat: 2.8g | Protein: 4.3g | Cholesterol: 19mg

INGREDIENTS

- 2 1/2 cups warm water (110 degrees F/45 degrees C)
- 3 eggs
- 1 tablespoon active dry yeast
- 1 tablespoon salt
- 1/2 cup honey
- 8 cups unbleached all-purpose flour
- 4 tablespoons vegetable oil
- 1 tablespoon poppy seeds (optional)

DIRECTIONS

1. In a large bowl, sprinkle yeast over barely warm water. Beat in honey, oil, 2 eggs, and salt. Add the flour one cup at a time, beating after each addition, graduating to kneading with hands as dough thickens. Knead until smooth and elastic and no longer sticky, adding flour as needed. Cover with a damp clean cloth and let rise for 1 1/2 hours or until dough has doubled in bulk.
2. Punch down the risen dough and turn out onto floured board. Divide in half and knead each half for five minutes or so, adding flour as needed to keep from getting sticky. Divide each half into thirds and roll into long snake about 1 1/2 inches in diameter. Pinch the ends of the three snakes together firmly and braid from middle. Either leave as braid or form into a round braided loaf by bringing

ends together, curving braid into a circle, pinch ends together. Grease two baking trays and place finished braid or round on each. Cover with towel and let rise about one hour.

3. Preheat oven to 375 degrees F (190 degrees C).
4. Beat the remaining egg and brush a generous amount over each braid. Sprinkle with poppy seeds if desired.
5. Bake at 375 degrees F (190 degrees C) for about 40 minutes. Bread should have a nice hollow sound when thumped on the bottom. Cool on a rack for at least one hour before slicing.

HONEY WHEAT BREAD

Servings: 24 | Prep: 25m | Cooks: 35m | Total: 2h30m | Additional: 1h30m

NUTRITION FACTS

Calories: 156 | Carbohydrates: 24.5g | Fat: 4.8g | Protein: 4.6g | Cholesterol: 7mg

INGREDIENTS

- 1 (.25 ounce) package rapid rise yeast
- 1/4 cup honey
- 1 teaspoon white sugar
- 2 teaspoons salt
- 1/2 cup warm water (110 degrees F/45 degrees C)
- 2 cups whole wheat flour
- 1 (12 fluid ounce) can evaporated milk
- 3 cups bread flour
- 1/4 cup water
- 2 tablespoons butter
- 1/4 cup melted shortening

DIRECTIONS

1. Dissolve yeast and sugar in 1/2 cup warm water.
2. Combine milk, 1/4 cup water, shortening, honey, salt and wheat flour in food processor or bowl. Mix in yeast mixture, and let rest 15 minutes. Add bread flour, and process until dough forms a ball. Knead dough by processing an additional 80 seconds in food processor, or mix and knead by hand 10 minutes. Place the dough in a buttered bowl, and turn to coat. Cover the bowl with plastic wrap. Let dough rise for 45 minutes, or until almost doubled.
3. Punch down, and divide dough in half. Roll out each half, and pound out the bubbles. Form into loaves, and place in buttered 9x5 inch bread pans. Butter the tops of the dough, and cover loosely with plastic wrap. Let rise in a warm area until doubled; second rise should take about 30 minutes.

4. Place a small pan of water on the bottom shelf of the oven. Preheat oven to 375 degrees F (190 degrees C).
5. Bake for 25 to 35 minutes, or until tops are dark golden brown. Butter crusts while warm. Slice when cool.

HONEY CORNBREAD

Servings: 8 | Prep: 8m | Cooks: 25m | Total: 34m | Additional: 1m

NUTRITION FACTS

Calories: 358 | Carbohydrates: 41.8g | Fat: 19.5g | Protein: 5.1g | Cholesterol: 87mg

INGREDIENTS

- 1 cup all-purpose flour
- 1 cup heavy cream
- 1 cup yellow cornmeal
- 1/4 cup vegetable oil
- 1/4 cup white sugar
- 1/4 cup honey
- 1 tablespoon baking powder
- 2 eggs, lightly beaten

DIRECTIONS

1. Preheat oven to 400 degrees F (200 degrees C). Lightly grease a 9x9 inch baking pan.
2. n a large bowl, stir together flour, cornmeal, sugar and baking powder. Make a well in the center of the dry ingredients. Add the cream, oil, honey and eggs; stir to combine. Pour batter into prepared baking pan.
3. Bake in preheated oven for 20 to 25 minutes, until a toothpick inserted into center of pan comes out clean.

CHEESE GARLIC BISCUITS

Servings: 12 | Prep: 10m | Cooks: 15m | Total: 25m

NUTRITION FACTS

Calories: 191 | Carbohydrates: 15.1g | Fat: 12.3g | Protein: 5g | Cholesterol: 34mg

INGREDIENTS

* 1 3/4 cups all-purpose flour
* 1 cup milk
* 1/2 teaspoon salt
* 1 cup shredded Cheddar cheese
* 1/2 teaspoon baking powder
* 1/4 cup butter, melted
* 5 tablespoons butter
* 1 clove garlic, minced

DIRECTIONS

1. Preheat oven to 450 degrees F (230 degrees C).
2. In a large bowl, sift together flour, salt and baking powder. Cut in butter until mixture resembles coarse crumbs. Make a well in the center of flour mixture. Add the milk and cheddar cheese; stir to combine. Drop batter by spoonfuls onto an ungreased baking sheet.
3. Bake in preheated oven for 12 to 15 minutes, until lightly browned. While biscuits are baking mix melted butter and minced garlic. Brush garlic butter over hot baked biscuits.

PUMPKIN MUFFINS

Servings: 12 | Prep: 20m | Cooks: 25m | Total: 45m

NUTRITION FACTS

Calories: 383 | Carbohydrates: 60.7g | Fat: 14g | Protein: 5.3g | Cholesterol: 47mg

INGREDIENTS

* 1 small sugar pumpkin, seeded
* 2 teaspoons ground cinnamon
* 3 cups all-purpose flour
* 2 teaspoons ground nutmeg
* 2 cups white sugar
* 1 teaspoon ground allspice
* 2 teaspoons baking soda
* 1 teaspoon salt
* 1/2 teaspoon baking powder
* 2/3 cup vegetable oil
* 2 teaspoons ground cloves
* 3 eggs

DIRECTIONS

1. Preheat oven to 350 degrees F (175 degrees C). Grease 12 muffin cups or line with paper muffin liners.
2. Split pumpkin in half. Remove seeds and strings. Place on baking sheet, cut side down. Cover with foil and bake in preheated oven until tender, about 90 minutes. Remove pumpkin pulp and puree in blender. Measure out 2 cups pumpkin puree; set aside.
3. In a large bowl, stir together flour, sugar, baking soda, baking powder, cloves, cinnamon, nutmeg, allspice and salt. In a separate bowl, beat together 2 cups pumpkin puree, vegetable oil and eggs. Stir pumpkin mixture into flour mixture until smooth. Scoop batter into prepared muffin cups.
4. Bake in preheated oven for 20 to 25 minutes, until a toothpick inserted into the center of a muffin comes out clean.

SWEET CORN CAKE

Servings: 6 | Prep: 15m | Cooks: 1h | Total: 1h15m

NUTRITION FACTS

Calories: 273 | Carbohydrates: 27.9g | Fat: 18.1g | Protein: 2.6g | Cholesterol: 47mg

INGREDIENTS

- 1/2 cup butter, softened
- 1/3 cup white sugar
- 1/3 cup masa harina
- 2 tablespoons heavy whipping cream
- 1/4 cup water
- 1/4 teaspoon salt
- 1 1/2 cups frozen whole-kernel corn, thawed
- 1/2 teaspoon baking powder
- 1/4 cup cornmeal

DIRECTIONS

1. In a medium bowl beat butter until it is creamy. Add the Mexican corn flour and water and beat until well mixed.
2. Using a food processor, process thawed corn, but leave chunky. Stir into the butter mixture.
3. In a separate bowl, mix cornmeal, sugar, cream, salt, and baking powder. Add to corn flour mixture and stir to combine. Pour batter into an ungreased 8x8 inch baking pan. Smooth batter and cover with aluminum foil. Place pan into a 9x13 inch baking dish that is filled a third of the way with water.

4. Bake in a preheated 350 degree oven F (175 degrees C) oven for 50 to 60 minutes. Allow to cool for 10 minutes. Use an ice cream scoop for easy removal from pan.

ITALIAN BREAD USING A BREAD MACHINE
Servings: 20 | Prep: 20m | Cooks: 35m | Total: 3h20m | Additional: 2h25m

NUTRITION FACTS

Calories: 105 | Carbohydrates: 20.6g | Fat: 0.9g | Protein: 3.1g | Cholesterol: 9mg

INGREDIENTS

- 4 cups unbleached all-purpose flour
- 1 (.25 ounce) package active dry yeast
- 1 tablespoon light brown sugar
- 1 egg
- 1 1/3 cups warm water (110 degrees F/45 degrees C)
- 1 tablespoon water
- 1 1/2 teaspoons salt
- 2 tablespoons cornmeal
- 1 1/2 teaspoons olive oil

DIRECTIONS

1. Place flour, brown sugar, warm water, salt, olive oil and yeast in the pan of the bread machine in the order recommended by the manufacturer. Select dough cycle; press Start.
2. Deflate the dough and turn it out onto a lightly floured surface. Form dough into two loaves. Place the loaves seam side down on a cutting board generously sprinkled with cornmeal. Cover the loaves with a damp cloth and let rise, until doubled in volume about 40 minutes. Meanwhile, preheat oven to 375 degrees F (190 degrees C).
3. In a small bowl, beat together egg and 1 tablespoon water. Brush the risen loaves with egg mixture. Make a single long, quick cut down the center of the loaves with a sharp knife. Gently shake the cutting board to make sure that the loaves are not sticking. If they stick, use a spatula or pastry knife to loosen. Slide the loaves onto a baking sheet with one quick but careful motion.
4. Bake in preheated oven for 30 to 35 minutes, or until loaves sound hollow when tapped on the bottom.

PIZZA DOUGH
Servings: 16 | Prep: 20m | Cooks: 30m | Total: 2h | Additional: 1h10m

Calories: 202 | Carbohydrates: 37.8g | Fat: 2.6g | Protein: 6.3g | Cholesterol: 0mg

INGREDIENTS

- 1 (.25 ounce) package active dry yeast
- 1 tablespoon salt
- 1 tablespoon white sugar
- 1/2 cup whole wheat flour
- 2 1/2 cups warm water (110 degrees F)
- 5 1/2 cups bread flour
- 2 tablespoons olive oil

DIRECTIONS

1. In a large mixing bowl, dissolve yeast and sugar in the warm water. Let sit until creamy; about 10 minutes.
2. Stir the olive oil, whole wheat flour, salt and 4 cups of the bread flour into the yeast mixture. Mix in the remaining flour, 1/2 cup at a time, stirring well after each addition. When the dough has pulled together, turn it out onto a lightly floured surface and knead until smooth and elastic, about 8 minutes. Lightly oil a large mixing bowl, place the dough in the bowl and turn to coat with oil. Cover with a damp cloth and put in a warm place to rise until doubled in volume; about 1 hour.
3. Deflate the dough and turn it out onto a lightly floured surface. Divide the dough into three equal pieces and form into rounds. Cover the rounds and let them rest for about 10 minutes. Preheat oven to 425 degrees F (220 degrees C).
4. Use a rolling pin to roll the dough into the desired shape, cover it with your favorite toppings and bake at 425 degrees F (220 degrees C) for about 20 minutes or until the crust and cheese are golden brown.

MOCHA CHOCOLATE CHIP BANANA MUFFINS

Servings: 18 | Prep: 10m | Cooks: 25m | Total: 35m

NUTRITION FACTS

Calories: 267 | Carbohydrates: 36.5g | Fat: 13.3g | Protein: 2.7g | Cholesterol: 10mg

INGREDIENTS

- 1 cup margarine

- 1 teaspoon vanilla extract
- 1 1/4 cups white sugar
- 2 1/4 cups all-purpose flour
- 1 egg
- 1/4 teaspoon salt
- 3 ripe bananas
- 1 teaspoon baking powder
- 1 tablespoon instant coffee granules, dissolved in
- 1 teaspoon baking soda
- 1 tablespoon water
- 1 cup semisweet chocolate chips

DIRECTIONS

1. Preheat oven to 350 degrees F (175 degrees C).
2. Blend butter or margarine, sugar, egg, banana, dissolved coffee, and vanilla in food processor for 2 minutes. Add flour, salt, baking powder, and soda, and blend just until flour disappears. Add chocolate chips and mix in with wooden spoon. Spoon mixture into 15 to 18 paper-lined muffin cups.
3. Bake for 25 minutes. Cool on wire racks.

JANINE'S BEST BANANA BREAD

Servings: 10 | Prep: 15m | Cooks: 1h | Total: 1h15m

NUTRITION FACTS

Calories: 248 | Carbohydrates: 47.2g | Fat: 5.5g | Protein: 3.6g | Cholesterol: 31mg

INGREDIENTS

- 1/4 cup butter, softened
- 2 cups all-purpose flour
- 1 cup white sugar
- 1 teaspoon baking soda
- 1 egg
- 1/2 teaspoon salt
- 3 ripe bananas, mashed

DIRECTIONS

1. Preheat oven to 350 degrees F (175 degrees C). Lightly grease an 8x4 inch loaf pan.
2. In a large bowl, cream together butter and sugar. Beat in the egg and mashed bananas. Mix in flour, baking soda and salt just until combined. Pour into prepared loaf pan.
3. Bake in preheated oven for 1 hour. If top begins to brown too quickly, decrease heat slightly. Center should be soft and chewy, while the outside, crisp and crunchy.

WHOLE WHEAT BEER BREAD

Servings: 12 | Prep: 10m | Cooks: 50m | Total: 1h

NUTRITION FACTS

Calories: 144 | Carbohydrates: 30.2g | Fat: 0.4g | Protein: 3.8g | Cholesterol: 0mg

INGREDIENTS

- 1 1/2 cups all-purpose flour
- 1 1/2 teaspoons salt
- 1 1/2 cups whole wheat flour
- 1/3 cup packed brown sugar
- 4 1/2 teaspoons baking powder
- 1 (12 fluid ounce) can or bottle beer

DIRECTIONS

1. Preheat oven to 350 degrees F (175 degrees C). Lightly grease a 9x5 inch loaf pan.
2. In a large mixing bowl, combine all-purpose flour, whole wheat flour, baking powder, salt and brown sugar. Pour in beer, stir until a stiff batter is formed. It may be necessary to mix dough with your hands. Scrape dough into prepared loaf pan.
3. Bake in preheated oven for 50 to 60 minutes, until a toothpick inserted into center of the loaf comes out clean.

CINNAMON ROLLS

Servings: 24 | Prep: 30m | Cooks: 25m | Total: 2h25m | Additional: 1h30m

NUTRITION FACTS

Calories: 331 | Carbohydrates: 55.5g | Fat: 10.4g | Protein: 4.7g | Cholesterol: 42mg

INGREDIENTS

- 1 cup milk
- 2 teaspoons ground cinnamon
- 1/2 cup butter
- 2 cups dark brown sugar

- 1 cup water
- 1/2 cup butter, softened
- 1 tablespoon active dry yeast
- 2 cups confectioners' sugar
- 1 cup white sugar
- 1 (3 ounce) package cream cheese, softened
- 1 teaspoon salt
- 1 tablespoon butter, softened
- 2 eggs
- 1/2 teaspoon vanilla extract
- 6 cups all-purpose flour
- 3 tablespoons milk

DIRECTIONS

1. Warm the milk in a small saucepan until it bubbles, then remove from heat. Mix in the butter; stir until melted. Add water and let cool until lukewarm.
2. In a large bowl, combine the milk mixture, yeast, white sugar, salt, eggs and 2 cups flour; stir well to combine. Stir in the remaining flour, 1/2 cup at a time, beating well after each addition. When the dough has pulled together, turn it out onto a lightly floured surface and knead until smooth and elastic, about 8 minutes.
3. Divide dough into two pieces. Roll each piece into a 12x9 inch rectangle. In a bowl, stir together the cinnamon and brown sugar. Spread each piece with half of the butter, half of the brown sugar and cinnamon mixture. Roll up dough, using a little water to seal the seam.
4. Cut each roll into 12 slices using a very sharp knife or dental floss. Place rolls onto two 9x13 inch greased baking pans. Cover and let rise until almost doubled, about 1 hour. Meanwhile, preheat oven to 375 degrees F (190 degrees C).
5. Bake in preheated oven for 20 to 25 minutes until golden brown.
6. To make frosting; combine confectioner's sugar, cream cheese, butter and vanilla. Add milk gradually until frosting reaches a spreading consistency. Spread over warm (but not hot) cinnamon rolls.

ENGLISH MUFFINS

Servings: 18 | Prep: 25m | Cooks: 20m | Total: 2h15m | Additional: 1h30m

NUTRITION FACTS

Calories: 190 | Carbohydrates: 34g | Fat: 3.5g | Protein: 4.9g | Cholesterol: 1mg

INGREDIENTS

- 1 cup milk

- 1/4 cup melted shortening
- 2 tablespoons white sugar
- 6 cups all-purpose flour
- 1 (.25 ounce) package active dry yeast
- 1 teaspoon salt
- 1 cup warm water (110 degrees F/45 degrees C)

DIRECTIONS

1. Warm the milk in a small saucepan until it bubbles, then remove from heat. Mix in the sugar, stirring until dissolved. Let cool until lukewarm. In a small bowl, dissolve yeast in warm water. Let stand until creamy, about 10 minutes.
2. In a large bowl, combine the milk, yeast mixture, shortening and 3 cups flour. Beat until smooth. Add salt and rest of flour, or enough to make a soft dough. Knead. Place in greased bowl, cover, and let rise.
3. Punch down. Roll out to about 1/2 inch thick. Cut rounds with biscuit cutter, drinking glass, or empty tuna can. Sprinkle waxed paper with cornmeal and set the rounds on this to rise. Dust tops of muffins with cornmeal also. Cover and let rise 1/2 hour.
4. Heat greased griddle. Cook muffins on griddle about 10 minutes on each side on medium heat. Keep baked muffins in a warm oven until all have been cooked. Allow to cool and place in plastic bags for storage. To use, split and toast. Great with orange butter, or cream cheese and jam.

WHOLE WHEAT BANANA NUT BREAD
Servings: 12 | Prep: 15m | Cooks: 55m | Total: 1h10m

NUTRITION FACTS

Calories: 218 | Carbohydrates: 29.4g | Fat: 10.5g | Protein: 4.4g | Cholesterol: 31mg

INGREDIENTS

- 1/3 cup vegetable oil
- 1 3/4 cups whole wheat flour
- 1/2 cup honey
- 1/2 teaspoon salt
- 1 teaspoon vanilla extract
- 1 teaspoon baking soda
- 2 eggs
- 1/4 cup hot water
- 1 cup mashed bananas

- 1/2 cup chopped walnuts

DIRECTIONS

1. Preheat oven to 325 degrees F (165 degrees C). Grease a 9x5-inch loaf pan.
2. In a large bowl, beat oil and honey together. Add eggs, and mix well. Stir in bananas and vanilla. Stir in flour and salt. Add baking soda to hot water, stir to mix, and then add to batter. Blend in chopped nuts. Spread batter into prepared pan.
3. Bake until a toothpick inserted in the center of the loaf comes out clean, 55 to 60 minutes. Cool on wire rack for 1/2 hour before slicing.

SOFT, MOIST AND GOOEY CINNAMON BUNS
Servings: 24 | Prep: 15m | Cooks: 20m | Total: 3h35m | Additional: 3h

NUTRITION FACTS

Calories: 165 | Carbohydrates: 21.2g | Fat: 8.9g | Protein: 1.1g | Cholesterol: 29mg

INGREDIENTS

- 1 cup milk
- 1/2 cup butter, softened
- 1 egg, beaten
- 1 cup packed brown sugar
- 4 tablespoons melted butter
- 2 teaspoons ground cinnamon
- 4 tablespoons water
- 1/4 cup chopped walnuts (optional)
- 1/2 (3.5 ounce) package instant vanilla pudding mix
- 1/4 cup raisins (optional)
- 4 cups bread flour
- 1 teaspoon milk
- 1 tablespoon white sugar
- 1 1/2 cups confectioners' sugar
- 1/2 teaspoon salt
- 4 tablespoons butter, softened
- 2 1/4 teaspoons bread machine yeast
- 1 teaspoon vanilla extract

DIRECTIONS

1. In a bread machine pan, place the milk, beaten egg, melted butter, water, vanilla pudding mix, bread flour, sugar, salt and yeast in the order recommended by the manufacturer. Select the Dough cycle.
2. When cycle is finished, remove the dough, and knead for 3 to 5 minutes. Roll out to a large rectangle.
3. Mix together the softened butter, brown sugar and cinnamon. Spread over dough. Sprinkle with chopped walnuts and raisins, if desired. Starting with the widest end, roll the dough into a log. Pinch to seal seams. Cut into 1/2 inch to 1 inch slices, and place in a greased 9x13 inch pan. Place in a draft-free space, and allow to rise until doubled.
4. Preheat the oven to 350 degrees F (175 degrees C). Bake for 15 to 20 minutes. To make frosting, mix the milk, confectioners sugar, softened butter and vanilla in a small bowl. Spread over warm cinnamon rolls.

SWEET CORN BREAD

Servings: 9 | Prep: 10m | Cooks: 20m | Total: 40m | Additional: 10m

NUTRITION FACTS

Calories: 241 | Carbohydrates: 29.9g | Fat: 11.6g | Protein: 4.4g | Cholesterol: 46mg

INGREDIENTS

- 1 cup all-purpose flour
- 1/2 teaspoon salt
- 1 cup cornmeal
- 1 egg, lightly beaten
- 1/4 cup white sugar
- 1 cup sour cream
- 1/2 teaspoon baking powder
- 1/3 cup milk
- 1/2 teaspoon baking soda
- 1/4 cup butter, melted
- 1 cup all-purpose flour

DIRECTIONS

1. Preheat oven to 400 degrees F (205 degrees C). Lightly grease an 8-inch square baking dish.
2. Combine flour, cornmeal, sugar, baking powder, baking soda, and salt in a large bowl. Mix egg, sour cream, milk, and butter in a small bowl. Fold egg mixture into flour mixture until just moistened; pour into prepared baking dish.
3. Bake in preheated oven until a toothpick inserted near the center comes out clean, 20 to 25 minutes. Serve warm.

DELICIOUS PUMPKIN BREAD

Servings: 24 | Prep: 10m | Cooks: 1h | Total: 1h10m

NUTRITION FACTS

Calories: 275 | Carbohydrates: 40.1g | Fat: 11.9g | Protein: 3.4g | Cholesterol: 31mg

INGREDIENTS

- 3 1/4 cups all-purpose flour
- 2 cups solid pack pumpkin puree
- 3 cups white sugar
- 2/3 cup water
- 2 teaspoons baking soda
- 1 cup vegetable oil
- 1 1/2 teaspoons salt
- 4 eggs
- 1 teaspoon ground nutmeg
- 1/2 cup chopped walnuts (optional)
- 1 teaspoon ground cinnamon

DIRECTIONS

1. Grease and flour three 7 x 3 inch pans. Preheat oven to 350 degrees F (175 degrees C).
2. Measure flour, sugar, baking soda, salt, and spices into a large bowl. Stir to blend. Add pumpkin, water, vegetable oil, eggs, and nuts. Beat until well combined. Pour batter into prepared pans.
3. Bake for approximately 1 hour.

EASY APPLE CINNAMON MUFFINS

Servings: 6 | Prep: 20m | Cooks: 25m | Total: 45m

NUTRITION FACTS

Calories: 589 | Carbohydrates: 79g | Fat: 29g | Protein: 5.8g | Cholesterol: 73mg

INGREDIENTS

- 1 1/2 cups all-purpose flour
- 1/3 cup milk

- 3/4 cup white sugar
- 2 apples - peeled, cored and chopped
- 1/2 teaspoon salt
- 1/2 cup white sugar
- 2 teaspoons baking powder
- 1/3 cup all-purpose flour
- 1 teaspoon ground cinnamon
- 1/2 cup butter, cubed
- 1/3 cup vegetable oil
- 1 1/2 teaspoons ground cinnamon
- 1 egg

DIRECTIONS

1. Preheat oven to 400 degrees F (200 degrees C). Grease six muffin cups or line with paper muffin liners.
2. Stir together 1 1/2 cup flour, 3/4 cup sugar, salt, baking powder and 1 teaspoon cinnamon. Mix in oil, egg and milk. Fold in apples. Spoon batter into prepared muffin cups, filling to the top of the cup.
3. In a small bowl, stir together 1/2 cup sugar, 1/3 cup flour, butter and 1 1/2 teaspoons cinnamon. Mix together with fork and sprinkle over unbaked muffins.
4. Bake in preheated oven for 20 to 25 minutes, until a toothpick inserted into center of a muffin comes out clean.

BREAD MACHINE PIZZA DOUGH

Servings: 6 | Prep: 10m | Cooks: 24m | Total: 2h34m | Additional: 2h

NUTRITION FACTS

Calories: 262 | Carbohydrates: 46g | Fat: 4.4g | Protein: 6.2g | Cholesterol: 10mg

INGREDIENTS

- 1 cup flat beer
- 1 teaspoon salt
- 2 tablespoons butter
- 2 1/2 cups all-purpose flour
- 2 tablespoons sugar
- 2 1/4 teaspoons yeast

DIRECTIONS

1. Put beer, butter, sugar, salt, flour, and yeast in a bread machine in the order recommended by the manufacturer. Select Dough setting, and press Start.
2. Remove dough from bread machine when cycle is complete. Roll or press dough to cover a prepared pizza pan. Brush lightly with olive oil. Cover and let stand 15 minutes.
3. Preheat oven to 400 degrees F (200 degrees C).
4. Spread sauce and toppings on top of dough. Bake until crust is lightly brown and crispy on the outside, about 24 minutes.

HONEY OF AN OATMEAL BREAD
Servings: 10 | Prep: 5m | Cooks: 3h | Total: 3h5m

NUTRITION FACTS

Calories: 170 | Carbohydrates: 33.1g | Fat: 2.2g | Protein: 4.5g | Cholesterol: 0mg

INGREDIENTS

- 1 cup water
- 1/2 cup rolled oats
- 1 tablespoon vegetable oil
- 2 1/3 cups bread flour
- 1/4 cup honey
- 1 teaspoon active dry yeast
- 1 teaspoon salt

DIRECTIONS

1. Place ingredients in bread machine pan in the order suggested by the manufacturer.
2. Select Light Crust or Basic setting, and press Start.

ANGIE'S PERFECT DINNER ROLLS
Servings: 36 | Prep: 25m | Cooks: 10m | Total: 4h35m | Additional: 4h

NUTRITION FACTS

Calories: 158 | Carbohydrates: 22.3g | Fat: 6g | Protein: 3.6g | Cholesterol: 25mg

INGREDIENTS

- 2 1/2 cups warm milk
- 1/2 cup butter, softened
- 4 teaspoons active dry yeast
- 2 teaspoons salt
- 1/2 cup sugar
- 7 cups all-purpose flour, or as needed
- 2 eggs
- 1/2 cup butter, melted

DIRECTIONS

1. Pour milk into a large mixing bowl, and sprinkle yeast over the surface. Allow to rest for 5 minutes. Beat in the sugar, eggs, 1/2 cup butter, and salt; blend thoroughly. Gradually stir in the flour to make a soft dough. Cover bowl, and set in a warm place until dough doubles in size, about 1 hour.
2. Punch down the dough, cover the bowl, and allow to rise again. Repeat this step two more times.
3. Break off 2 to 3 inch size pieces of dough, roll lightly into round shape, and place in prepared baking dish, edges touching. Repeat to make 36 dough balls. Cover and let rise until doubled in size.
4. Preheat oven to 400 degrees F (200 degrees C). Lightly grease a 9x13 inch baking dish.
5. Bake rolls in preheated oven until tops turn golden brown, 10 to 15 minutes. When rolls are finished baking, drizzle melted butter over the top, and serve warm.

OATMEAL CHOCOLATE CHIP MUFFINS

Servings: 12 | Prep: 20m | Cooks: 25m | Total: 45m

NUTRITION FACTS

Calories: 345 | Carbohydrates: 38.7g | Fat: 20.4g | Protein: 5.1g | Cholesterol: 18mg

INGREDIENTS

- 1 1/4 cups quick cooking oats
- 3/4 cup semisweet chocolate chips
- 1 1/4 cups milk
- 1 cup chopped pecans
- 1 egg
- 1 1/4 cups all-purpose flour
- 1/2 cup vegetable oil
- 4 teaspoons baking powder

- 3/4 cup packed brown sugar
- 1 teaspoon salt

DIRECTIONS

1. Combine oats and milk and allow to stand for 15 minutes. Preheat oven to 400 degrees F (205 degrees C). Grease each cup of one 12-cup muffin tin.
2. Stir egg, oil, 1/2 cup of the brown sugar, chocolate chips and 1/2 cup of the pecans into the oat and milk mixture.
3. Combine flour, baking powder and salt. Add oat mixture to flour mixture, stirring until just moist. Fill each cup of one 12-cup muffin tin 2/3 full. Sprinkle tops with the remaining brown sugar and pecans.
4. Bake at 400 degrees F (205 degrees C) for 20 to 25 minutes.

CHEDDAR BISCUITS

Servings: 8 | Prep: 15m | Cooks: 20m | Total: 35m

NUTRITION FACTS

Calories: 214 | Carbohydrates: 19.9g | Fat: 12.3g | Protein: 6.4g | Cholesterol: 16mg

INGREDIENTS

- 2 cups biscuit baking mix
- 2 tablespoons margarine, melted
- 1 cup shredded Cheddar cheese
- 2 teaspoons dried parsley
- 2/3 cup milk
- 1 teaspoon garlic salt
- 1/2 teaspoon garlic powder

DIRECTIONS

1. Preheat oven to 400 degrees F (205 degrees C). Grease a cookie sheet, or line with parchment paper.
2. In a large bowl, combine baking mix, Cheddar cheese, and garlic powder. Stir in milk. Drop batter by heaping tablespoonfuls onto prepared cookie sheet.
3. Bake in preheated oven for 10 minutes. Brush biscuits with melted margarine, and sprinkle with parsley and garlic salt. Bake for 5 more minutes, or until lightly browned on the bottom.

CORNBREAD MUFFINS

Servings: 12 | Prep: 10m | Cooks: 25m | Total: 35m

NUTRITION FACTS

Calories: 243 | Carbohydrates: 37.4g | Fat: 9.2g | Protein: 4g | Cholesterol: 52mg

INGREDIENTS

- 1/2 cup butter, softened
- 1 1/2 cups all-purpose flour
- 2/3 cup white sugar
- 3/4 cup cornmeal
- 1/4 cup honey
- 1/2 teaspoon baking powder
- 2 eggs
- 1/2 cup milk
- 1/2 teaspoon salt
- 3/4 cup frozen corn kernels, thawed

DIRECTIONS

1. Preheat oven to 400 degrees F (200 degrees C). Grease or line 12 muffin cups.
2. In a large bowl, cream together butter, sugar, honey, eggs and salt. Mix in flour, cornmeal and baking powder; blend thoroughly. Stir in milk and corn. Pour or spoon batter into prepared muffin cups.
3. Bake in preheated oven for 20 to 25 minutes, or until a toothpick inserted into center of a muffin comes out clean.

CLASSIC DINNER ROLLS

Servings: 12 | Prep: 40m | Cooks: 20m | Total: 1h30m | Additional: 30m

NUTRITION FACTS

Calories: 106 | Carbohydrates: 18.5g | Fat: 2.3g | Protein: 2.5g | Cholesterol: 6mg

INGREDIENTS

- 2 cups all-purpose flour, or more if needed
- 1/2 cup milk
- 1 envelope Fleischmann's® RapidRise Yeast
- 1/4 cup water

- 2 tablespoons sugar
- 2 tablespoons butter OR margarine
- 1/2 teaspoon salt

DIRECTIONS

1. Combine 3/4 cup flour, undissolved yeast, sugar and salt in a large bowl. Heat milk, water and butter until very warm (120 degrees to 130 degrees F). Add to flour mixture. Beat 2 minutes at medium speed of electric mixer, scraping bowl occasionally. Add 1/4 cup flour; beat 2 minutes at high speed. Stir in enough remaining flour to make soft dough. Knead on lightly floured surface until smooth and elastic, about 8 to 10 minutes. Cover; let rest 10 minutes.
2. Divide dough into 12 equal pieces; shape into balls. Place in greased 8-inch round pan. Cover; let rise in warm, draft-free place until doubled in size, about 30 minutes.
3. Bake in preheated 375 degrees F oven for 20 minutes or until done. Remove from pan; brush with additional melted butter, if desired. Serve warm.

BELLE'S HAMBURGER BUNS

Servings: 12 | Prep: 2h | Cooks: 20m | Total: 2h20m

NUTRITION FACTS

Calories: 246 | Carbohydrates: 46g | Fat: 3.3g | Protein: 7.1g | Cholesterol: 24mg

INGREDIENTS

- 1 cup milk
- 5 1/2 cups all-purpose flour
- 1 cup water
- 1 (.25 ounce) envelope active dry yeast
- 2 tablespoons butter
- 1 egg yolk
- 1 tablespoon white sugar
- 1 tablespoon water
- 1 1/2 teaspoons salt

DIRECTIONS

1. Combine the milk, 1 cup of water, butter, sugar and salt in a saucepan. Bring to a boil then remove from the heat and let stand until lukewarm. If the mixture is too hot, it will kill the yeast.

2. In a large bowl, stir together the flour and yeast. Pour in wet ingredients and stir until the dough starts to pull together. If you have a stand mixer, use the dough hook to mix for about 8 minutes. If not, knead the dough on a floured surface for about 10 minutes. Place the dough in a greased bowl, turning to coat. Cover and let stand until doubled in size, about 1 hour.

3. Punch down the dough and divide into 12 portions They should be a little larger than a golf ball. Make tight balls out of the dough by pulling the dough tightly around and pinching it at the bottom. Place on a baking sheet lined with parchment paper or aluminum foil. After the rolls sit for a minute and relax, flatten each ball with the palm of your hand until it is 3 to 4 inches wide. You may want to oil your hand first. Set rolls aside until they double in size, about 20 minutes.

4. Preheat the oven to 400 degrees F (200 degrees C). Mix together the egg yolk and 1 tablespoon of water in a cup or small bowl. Brush onto the tops of the rolls. Position 2 oven racks so they are not too close to the top or bottom of the oven.

5. Bake for 10 minutes in the preheated oven. Remove the rolls from the oven and return them to different shelves so each one spends a little time on the top. Continue to bake for another 5 to 10 minutes, or until nicely browned on the top and bottom.

PEACH MUFFINS

Servings: 16 | Prep: 25m | Cooks: 25m | Total: 50m

NUTRITION FACTS

Calories: 351 | Carbohydrates: 44.3g | Fat: 18.2g | Protein: 3.6g | Cholesterol: 35mg

INGREDIENTS

- 3 cups all-purpose flour
- 1 1/4 cups vegetable oil
- 1 tablespoon ground cinnamon
- 3 eggs, lightly beaten
- 1 teaspoon baking soda
- 2 cups white sugar
- 1 teaspoon salt
- 2 cups peeled, pitted, and chopped peaches

DIRECTIONS

1. Preheat oven to 400 degrees F (200 degrees C). Grease the bottoms and sides of 16 muffin cups, or line with paper liners.

2. In a large bowl, mix the flour, cinnamon, baking soda, and salt. In a separate bowl, mix the oil, eggs, and sugar. Stir the oil mixture into the flour mixture just until moist. Fold in the peaches. Spoon into the prepared muffin cups.

3. Bake 25 minutes in the preheated oven, until a toothpick inserted in the center of a muffin comes out clean. Cool 10 minutes before turning out onto wire racks to cool completely.

AMISH BREAD

Servings: 12 | Prep: 5m | Cooks: 3h | Total: 4h10m | Additional: 1h5m

NUTRITION FACTS

Calories: 58 | Carbohydrates: 4.3g | Fat: 4.7g | Protein: 0.1g | Cholesterol: 0mg

INGREDIENTS

- 2 3/4 cups bread flour
- 1/4 cup white sugar
- 1/4 cup canola oil
- 1/2 teaspoon salt
- 1 teaspoon active dry yeast
- 18 tablespoons warm water

DIRECTIONS

1. Place ingredients in the pan of the bread machine in the order recommended by the manufacturer. Select White Bread cycle; press Start.
2. When the dough has raised once and second cycle of kneading begins, turn machine off. Reset by pressing Start once again. This gives the dough two full raising cycles before the final raising cycle prior to baking.

ITALIAN BREAD BOWLS

Servings: 8 | Prep: 30m | Cooks: 30m | Total: 2h15m | Additional: 1h15m

NUTRITION FACTS

Calories: 439 | Carbohydrates: 85g | Fat: 4.6g | Protein: 12.5g | Cholesterol: 0mg

INGREDIENTS

- 2 (.25 ounce) packages active dry yeast
- 7 cups all-purpose flour
- 2 1/2 cups warm water (110 degrees F/45 degrees C)
- 1 tablespoon cornmeal

- 2 teaspoons salt
- 1 egg white
- 2 tablespoons vegetable oil
- 1 tablespoon water

DIRECTIONS

1. In a large bowl, dissolve yeast in warm water. Let stand until creamy, about 10 minutes.
2. Add salt, oil and 4 cups flour to the yeast mixture; beat well. Stir in the remaining flour, 1/2 cup at a time, beating well with an electric mixer at medium speed after each addition.
3. When the dough has pulled together, turn it out onto a lightly floured surface and knead until smooth and elastic, about 6 minutes. Lightly oil a large bowl, place the dough in the bowl and turn to coat with oil. Cover with a damp cloth and let rise in a warm place until doubled in volume, about 40 minutes.
4. Punch dough down, and divide into 8 equal portions. Shape each portion into a 4 inch round loaf. Place loaves on lightly greased baking sheets sprinkled with cornmeal. Cover and let rise in a warm place, free from drafts, until doubled in bulk, about 35 minutes.
5. Preheat oven to 400 degrees F (200 degrees C). In a small bowl, beat together egg white and 1 tablespoon water; lightly brush the loaves with half of this egg wash.
6. Bake in preheated oven for 15 minutes. Brush with remaining egg mixture, and bake 10 to 15 more minutes or until golden. Cool on wire racks.
7. Bake in preheated oven for 15 minutes. Brush with remaining egg mixture, and bake 10 to 15 more minutes or until golden. Cool on wire racks.

PEAS AND GUMBO

Servings: 4 | Prep: 10m | Cooks: 20m | Total: 30m

NUTRITION FACTS

Calories: 250 | Carbohydrates: 16.5g | Fat: 17.1g | Protein: 7.8g | Cholesterol: 175mg

INGREDIENTS

- 2/3 cup milk, room temperature
- 3 tablespoons clarified butter
- 1/2 cup packed all-purpose flour
- 1 tablespoon butter
- 3 large eggs, room temperature
- 1/2 Meyer lemon, juiced
- 1/4 teaspoon vanilla extract

- 1 tablespoon confectioners' sugar, or to taste
- 1/4 teaspoon salt

DIRECTIONS

1. Preheat oven to 425 degrees F (220 degrees C).
2. Blend milk, flour, eggs, vanilla extract, and salt together in a blender until batter is smooth.
3. Melt clarified butter in a 10-inch cast-iron skillet over high heat until bubbling; pour batter into the center of the skillet.
4. Bake in the preheated oven until puffed and golden, 20 to 25 minutes. Brush with 1 tablespoon butter, drizzle lemon juice over the top, and dust with confectioners' sugar.

CINNAMON BELGIAN WAFFLES

Servings: 3 | Prep: 10m | Cooks: 15m | Total: 25m

NUTRITION FACTS

Calories: 380 | Carbohydrates: 39.3g | Fat: 19.4g | Protein: 11.4g | Cholesterol: 181mg

INGREDIENTS

- 2 egg yolks
- 1/2 teaspoon baking soda
- 1 teaspoon vanilla extract
- 1/2 tablespoon white sugar
- 1 cup buttermilk
- 1/4 teaspoon salt
- 1/2 cup butter, melted
- 2 egg whites
- 1 cup all-purpose flour
- 1 pinch ground cinnamon
- 1 1/2 teaspoons baking powder

DIRECTIONS

1. Preheat your waffle iron.
2. In a medium bowl, whisk together the eggs, vanilla, buttermilk and butter until well blended. Combine the flour, baking powder, baking soda, sugar, salt and cinnamon; stir into the buttermilk

mixture. In a separate bowl, whip the egg whites with an electric mixer until stiff. Fold into the batter.

3. Spoon batter onto the hot waffle iron, close, and cook until golden brown. Waffles are usually done when the steam subsides.

BRAN FLAX MUFFINS

Servings: 15 | Prep: 15m | Cooks: 20m | Total: 35m

NUTRITION FACTS

Calories: 272 | Carbohydrates: 40.9g | Fat: 11g | Protein: 6.7g | Cholesterol: 25mg

INGREDIENTS

- 1 1/2 cups all-purpose flour
- 3/4 cup skim milk
- 3/4 cup ground flax seed
- 2 eggs, beaten
- 3/4 cup oat bran
- 1 teaspoon vanilla extract
- 1 cup brown sugar
- 2 tablespoons vegetable oil
- 2 teaspoons baking soda
- 2 cups shredded carrots
- 1 teaspoon baking powder
- 2 apples, peeled, shredded
- 1 teaspoon salt
- 1/2 cup raisins
- 2 teaspoons ground cinnamon
- 1 cup chopped mixed nuts

DIRECTIONS

1. Preheat oven to 350 degrees F (175 degrees C). Grease muffin pan or line with paper muffin liners.
2. In a large bowl, mix together flour, flax seed, oat bran, brown sugar, baking soda, baking powder, salt and cinnamon. Add the milk, eggs, vanilla and oil; mix until just blended. Stir in the carrots, apples, raisins and nuts. Fill prepared muffin cups 2/3 full with batter.
3. Bake at 350 F (175 degrees C) for 15 to 20 minutes, or until a toothpick inserted into the center of a muffin comes out clean.

EASY CREAM CHEESE DANISH

Servings: 10 | Prep: 10m | Cooks: 30m | Total: 40m

NUTRITION FACTS

Calories: 498 | Carbohydrates: 50.9g | Fat: 29g | Protein: 7.5g | Cholesterol: 53mg

INGREDIENTS

- 2 (10 ounce) cans refrigerated crescent roll dough
- 2 teaspoons sour cream
- 2 (8 ounce) packages cream cheese, diced
- 1 cup confectioners' sugar
- 3/4 cup white sugar
- 1 tablespoon milk
- 1 1/2 teaspoons lemon juice
- 1 tablespoon butter, softened
- 1 teaspoon vanilla extract

DIRECTIONS

1. Preheat oven to 350 degrees F (175 degrees C). Lightly grease a 9x13 inch baking pan.
2. Line bottom of baking pan with 1 can of crescent rolls. Pinch all seams together to seal.
3. In a large bowl, mix together cream cheese, white sugar, lemon juice, vanilla extract and sour cream. Spread filling on top of rolls. Place second can of rolls on top of filling.
4. Bake in preheated oven for 20 to 30 minutes.
5. In a small bowl, stir together confectioners' sugar, milk and butter. After Danish has cooled, drizzle with icing.

BLUEBERRY SCONES

Servings: 12 | Prep: 15m | Cooks: 20m | Total: 35m

NUTRITION FACTS

Calories: 160 | Carbohydrates: 23.1g | Fat: 6.2g | Protein: 3.3g | Cholesterol: 31mg

INGREDIENTS

- 2 cups all-purpose flour
- 1/4 cup butter, chilled
- 1/4 cup packed brown sugar

- 1 cup fresh blueberries
- 1 tablespoon baking powder
- 3/4 cup half-and-half cream
- 1/4 teaspoon salt
- 1 egg

DIRECTIONS

1. Preheat oven to 375 degrees F (190 degrees C).
2. Cut butter into mixture of flour, sugar, baking powder, and salt. Add blueberries and toss to mix.
3. In separate bowl beat together cream and egg, and slowly pour into dry ingredients, stirring with rubber scraper until dough forms. Knead just until it comes together, 3 or 4 times. Don't overhandle.
4. Divide dough in half. On lightly floured board, shape each half into a 6-inch round. Cut into 6 wedges.
5. Bake on ungreased sheet about 20 minutes at 375 degrees F (190 degrees C). Serve warm.

AMUSEMENT PARK CORNBREAD

Servings: 8 | Prep: 10m | Cooks: 20m | Total: 30m

NUTRITION FACTS

Calories: 328 | Carbohydrates: 51.9g | Fat: 10.4g | Protein: 7.2g | Cholesterol: 70mg

INGREDIENTS

- 2/3 cup white sugar
- 2 cups all-purpose flour
- 1 teaspoon salt
- 1 tablespoon baking powder
- 1/3 cup butter, softened
- 3/4 cup cornmeal
- 1 teaspoon vanilla extract
- 1 1/3 cups milk
- 2 eggs

DIRECTIONS

1. Preheat oven to 400 degrees F (200 degrees C). Lightly grease an 8 inch skillet.
2. In a large bowl, beat together sugar, salt, butter and vanilla until creamy. Stir in eggs one at a time, beating well after each addition. In a separate bowl, mix together flour, baking powder and cornmeal. Stir flour mixture into egg mixture alternately with the milk. Beat well until blended.
3. Bake in preheated oven for 20 minutes, or until golden brown. Serve warm.

MAMA D'S ITALIAN BREAD

Servings: 36 | Prep: 20m | Cooks: 1h | Total: 2h50m | Additional: 1h30m

NUTRITION FACTS

Calories: 90 | Carbohydrates: 18.8g | Fat: 0.3g | Protein: 2.6g | Cholesterol: 0mg

INGREDIENTS

- 3 cups warm water (110 degrees F/45 degrees C)
- 1 tablespoon salt
- 1 teaspoon white sugar
- 7 cups all-purpose flour
- 1 tablespoon active dry yeast

DIRECTIONS

1. Add the sugar and yeast to the warm water and let proof.
2. Stir in 4 cups of flour and beat until smooth. Cover and let rest for 15 minutes.
3. Beat in the salt and then add enough remaining flour to make a stiff dough. Knead until as soft and smooth as a bambino's behind. Turn in a greased bowl, cover, and let double in size. (I put it in the oven with the light on - perfect rising temperature.)
4. Once doubled, punch down and divide into three. Place back in the bowl, cover, and let rise.
5. Once doubled again, punch down and form into three fat "footballs." Grease heavy cookie sheets and sprinkle with corn meal. Place the bread on the sheets, cover with a towel, and let rise.
6. Once risen, mist with water and place in a preheated 450 degrees F (230 degrees C) oven. Mist loaves with water and turn occasionally while they bake. Bread is done when golden brown and sounds hollow when tapped on the bottom.

MOIST CHOCOLATE MUFFINS

Servings: 12 | Prep: 15m | Cooks: 20m | Total: 1h35m | Additional: 1h

NUTRITION FACTS

Calories: 322 | Carbohydrates: 45.3g | Fat: 15g | Protein: 5.4g | Cholesterol: 18mg

INGREDIENTS

- 2 cups all-purpose flour
- 1 cup plain yogurt
- 1 cup white sugar
- 1/2 cup milk
- 3/4 cup chocolate chips
- 1 teaspoon vanilla extract
- 1/2 cup unsweetened cocoa powder
- 1/2 cup vegetable oil
- 1 teaspoon baking soda
- 1/4 cup chocolate chips
- 1 egg

DIRECTIONS

1. Preheat oven to 400 degrees F (200 degrees C). Grease 12 muffin cups or line with paper muffin liners.
2. Combine flour, sugar, 3/4 cup chocolate chips, cocoa powder, and baking soda in a large bowl. Whisk egg, yogurt, milk, vanilla, and vegetable oil in another bowl until smooth; pour into chocolate mixture and stir until batter is just blended. Fill prepared muffin cups 3/4 full and sprinkle with remaining 1/4 cup chocolate chips.
3. Bake in preheated oven until a toothpick inserted into the center comes out clean, about 20 minutes. Cool in the pans for 10 minutes before removing to cool completely on a wire rack.

SKY HIGH YORKSHIRE PUDDING

Servings: 12 | Prep: 15m | Cooks: 35m | Total: 50m

NUTRITION FACTS

Calories: 160 | Carbohydrates: 17.9g | Fat: 7.2g | Protein: 5.6g | Cholesterol: 65mg

INGREDIENTS

- 4 eggs
- 2 cups all-purpose flour
- 2 cups milk
- 1/4 cup vegetable oil

DIRECTIONS

1. Preheat the oven to 450 degrees F (230 degrees C).
2. In a large bowl, whisk together the eggs and milk until well blended. Whisk in the flour one cup at a time until frothy and well blended. Set aside.
3. Distribute the oil equally among 12 muffin cups, a little over a teaspoon per cup. Place in the oven for 5 to 10 minutes, until smoking. Remove from the oven and quickly ladle about 1/4 cup of batter into each cup.
4. Bake for 30 to 35 minutes in the preheated oven. Serve immediately. I turn my oven off and leave the door partially open with the yorkies inside to keep them from deflating while waiting for everyone to ask for seconds.

BELGIAN WAFFLES

Servings: 8 | Prep: 15m | Cooks: 20m | Total: 1h35m | Additional: 1h

NUTRITION FACTS

Calories: 506 | Carbohydrates: 65.3g | Fat: 21.4g | Protein: 12.3g | Cholesterol: 130mg

INGREDIENTS

- 1 (.25 ounce) package active dry yeast
- 1/2 cup white sugar
- 1/4 cup warm milk (110 degrees F/45 degrees C)
- 1 1/2 teaspoons salt
- 3 egg yolks
- 2 teaspoons vanilla extract
- 2 3/4 cups warm milk (110 degrees F/45 degrees C)
- 4 cups all-purpose flour
- 3/4 cup butter, melted and cooled to lukewarm
- 3 egg whites

DIRECTIONS

1. In a small bowl, dissolve yeast in 1/4 cup warm milk. Let stand until creamy, about 10 minutes.
2. In a large bowl, whisk together the egg yolks, 1/4 cup of the warm milk and the melted butter. Stir in the yeast mixture, sugar, salt and vanilla. Stir in the remaining 2 1/2 cups milk alternately with the flour, ending with the flour. Beat the egg whites until they form soft peaks; fold into the batter. Cover the bowl tightly with plastic wrap. Let rise in a warm place until doubled in volume, about 1 hour.

3. Preheat the waffle iron. Brush with oil and spoon about 1/2 cup (or as recommended by manufacturer) onto center of iron. Close the lid and bake until it stops steaming and the waffle is golden brown. Serve immediately or keep warm in 200 degree oven.

HONEY WHEAT SANDWICH ROLLS

Servings: 14 | Prep: 30m | Cooks: 15m | Total: 2h45m | Additional: 2h

NUTRITION FACTS

Calories: 191 | Carbohydrates: 31.9g | Fat: 4.7g | Protein: 5.8g | Cholesterol: 24mg

INGREDIENTS

- 1 1/4 cups warm milk
- 2 3/4 cups bread flour
- 1 egg, beaten
- 1 cup whole wheat flour
- 2 tablespoons butter, softened
- 1 1/4 teaspoons bread machine yeast
- 1/4 cup honey
- 2 tablespoons butter, melted
- 3/4 teaspoon salt

DIRECTIONS

1. Place ingredients in the pan of the bread machine in the order recommended by the manufacturer. Select dough cycle; press start.
2. When dough cycle has finished, turn dough out onto a lightly floured surface and roll out 3/4 inch thick. Cut out rolls with a 3 to 4 inch diameter biscuit cutter. Place on lightly greased cookie sheets; cover and let rise until doubled, about 1 hour. Meanwhile, preheat oven to 350 degrees F (175 degrees C).
3. Bake in preheated oven for 10 to 15 minutes. When rolls are finished baking, brush with melted butter.

AUNT NORMA'S RHUBARB MUFFINS

Servings: 24 | Prep: 15m | Cooks: 25m | Total: 50m | Additional: 10m

NUTRITION FACTS

Calories: 157 | Carbohydrates: 21.5g | Fat: 7.1g | Protein: 2.4g | Cholesterol: 9mg

INGREDIENTS

- 2 1/2 cups flour
- 1 teaspoon vanilla extract
- 1 teaspoon baking soda
- 1 cup buttermilk
- 1 teaspoon baking powder
- 1 1/2 cups diced rhubarb
- 1/2 teaspoon salt
- 1/2 cup chopped walnuts
- 1 1/4 cups brown sugar
- 1 tablespoon melted butter
- 1/2 cup vegetable oil
- 1/3 cup white sugar
- 1 egg
- 1 teaspoon ground cinnamon

DIRECTIONS

1. Preheat the oven to 350 degrees F (175 degrees C). Grease two 12 cup muffin pans or line with paper cups.
2. In a medium bowl, stir together the flour, baking soda, baking powder and salt. In a separate bowl, beat the brown sugar, oil, egg, vanilla and buttermilk with an electric mixer until smooth. Pour in the dry ingredients and mix by hand just until blended. Stir in the rhubarb and walnuts. Spoon the batter into the prepared cups, filling almost to the top. In a small bowl, stir together the melted butter, white sugar and cinnamon; sprinkle about 1 teaspoon of this mixture on top of each muffin.
3. Bake in the preheated oven until the tops of the muffins spring back when lightly pressed, about 25 minutes. Cool in the pans for at least 10 minutes before removing.

PORTUGUESE SWEET BREAD

Servings: 12 | Prep: 5m | Cooks: 3h | Total: 3h5m

NUTRITION FACTS

Calories: 56 | Carbohydrates: 6.9g | Fat: 2.6g | Protein: 1.5g | Cholesterol: 17mg

INGREDIENTS

- 1 cup milk
- 3/4 teaspoon salt
- 1 egg
- 3 cups bread flour
- 2 tablespoons margarine
- 2 1/2 teaspoons active dry yeast
- 1/3 cup white sugar

DIRECTIONS

1. Add ingredients in order suggested by your manufacturer.
2. Select "sweet bread" setting.

LEMON ZUCCHINI BREAD

Servings: 12 | Prep: 15m | Cooks: 45m | Total: 1h

NUTRITION FACTS

Calories: 195 | Carbohydrates: 25.2g | Fat: 9.7g | Protein: 2.3g | Cholesterol: 16mg

INGREDIENTS

- 1 1/2 cups shredded zucchini
- 1/2 teaspoon salt
- 3/4 cup white sugar
- 1/2 teaspoon baking soda
- 1 egg
- 1/4 teaspoon baking powder
- 1/2 cup vegetable oil
- 1 teaspoon ground cinnamon
- 1 1/2 cups all-purpose flour
- 2 teaspoons lemon zest

DIRECTIONS

1. Preheat oven to 325 degrees F (165 degrees C). Grease an 8x4 inch loaf pan.
2. In a bowl, beat together the zucchini, sugar, egg, and oil. In a separate bowl, sift together the flour, salt, baking soda, and baking powder; stir in the cinnamon and lemon zest. Stir the flour mixture into the zucchini mixture just until blended. Pour the batter into the prepared pan.
3. Bake 45 minutes in the preheated oven, until a knife inserted in the center comes out clean. Remove from heat, and cool about 10 minutes before turning out onto a wire rack to cool completely.

PUMPKIN PIE BREAD

Servings: 24 | Prep: 15m | Cooks: 1h | Total: 1h15m

NUTRITION FACTS

Calories: 263 | Carbohydrates: 40.6g | Fat: 10.3g | Protein: 3.1g | Cholesterol: 31mg

INGREDIENTS

- 3 1/2 cups all-purpose flour
- 3 cups white sugar
- 2 teaspoons baking soda
- 1 cup vegetable oil
- 1 teaspoon baking powder
- 4 eggs
- 3 teaspoons pumpkin pie spice
- 1 (15 ounce) can pumpkin puree
- 1 teaspoon salt
- 1/2 cup water

DIRECTIONS

1. Preheat oven to 350 degrees F (175 degrees C). Grease two 9x5 inch loaf pans. Sift together the flour, baking soda, baking powder, salt, and pumpkin pie spice. Set aside.
2. In a large bowl, beat together sugar, oil, eggs, and pumpkin. Stir in flour mixture alternately with water. Divide batter evenly between the prepared pans.
3. Bake in the preheated oven for 60 to 70 minutes, or until a toothpick inserted into the center comes out clean. For best flavor, store wrapped in plastic wrap at room temperature for a full day before serving.

RASPBERRY LEMON MUFFINS

Servings: 12 | Prep: 15m | Cooks: 15m | Total: 30m

NUTRITION FACTS

Calories: 175 | Carbohydrates: 33g | Fat: 3.8g | Protein: 2.9g | Cholesterol: 1mg

INGREDIENTS

- 1/2 cup plain yogurt
- 3/4 cup white sugar
- 3 tablespoons vegetable oil

- 2 teaspoons baking powder
- 1 tablespoon lemon juice
- 1/4 teaspoon salt
- 2 egg whites
- 1 teaspoon grated lemon zest
- 1/2 teaspoon lemon extract (optional)
- 1 cup frozen raspberries
- 1 1/2 cups all-purpose flour
- 2 tablespoons white sugar for decoration (optional)

DIRECTIONS

1. Preheat the oven to 400 degrees F (200 degrees C). Grease a 12 cup muffin tin, or line with paper liners.
2. In a large bowl, mix together the yogurt, oil, lemon juice, egg whites, and, if using, lemon extract. In a separate bowl, stir together the flour, 3/4 cup sugar, baking powder, salt, and lemon zest. Add the wet ingredients to the dry, and mix until just blended. Gently stir in the frozen raspberries. Spoon batter evenly into the prepared muffin cups. Sprinkle remaining sugar over the tops for decoration, if desired.
3. Bake for 15 to 17 minutes in the preheated oven, or until the top springs back when lightly touched. Cool muffins in the tin on a wire rack.

LIGHTER BANANA MUFFINS

Servings: 10 | Prep: 15m | Cooks: 25m | Total: 40m

NUTRITION FACTS

Calories: 195 | Carbohydrates: 42.2g | Fat: 1.4g | Protein: 4.2g | Cholesterol: 37mg

INGREDIENTS

- 2 eggs, beaten
- 1 teaspoon salt
- 3 very ripe bananas, mashed
- 3/4 cup white sugar
- 2 cups all-purpose flour
- 1 teaspoon baking soda

DIRECTIONS

1. Preheat oven to 350 degrees F (175 degrees C). Lightly grease or line 10 muffin cups.

2. In a medium bowl, combine eggs and bananas. In a separate bowl, mix together flour, salt, sugar and baking soda. Stir banana mixture into flour mixture. Fold in walnuts if desired. Pour batter into prepared muffin cups.
3. Bake in preheated oven for 20 to 25 minutes, or until a toothpick inserted into center of a muffin comes out clean.

FLAX AND SUNFLOWER SEED BREAD

Servings: 15 | Prep: 10m | Cooks: 30m | Total: 3h | Additional: 2h20m

NUTRITION FACTS

Calories: 140 | Carbohydrates: 22.7g | Fat: 4.2g | Protein: 4.2g | Cholesterol: 4mg

INGREDIENTS

- 1 1/3 cups water
- 1 teaspoon salt
- 2 tablespoons butter, softened
- 1 teaspoon active dry yeast
- 3 tablespoons honey
- 1/2 cup flax seeds
- 1 1/2 cups bread flour
- 1/2 cup sunflower seeds
- 1 1/3 cups whole wheat bread flour

DIRECTIONS

1. Place all ingredients (except sunflower seeds) in the pan of the bread machine in the order recommended by the manufacturer. Select basic white cycle; press start. Add the sunflower seeds when the alert sounds during the knead cycle.

CIABATTA BREAD

Servings: 24 | Prep: 30m | Cooks: 25m | Total: 1h55m | Additional: 1h

NUTRITION FACTS

Calories: 73 | Carbohydrates: 13.7g | Fat: 0.9g | Protein: 2.3g | Cholesterol: 0mg

INGREDIENTS

- 1 1/2 cups water

- 1 tablespoon olive oil
- 1 1/2 teaspoons salt
- 3 1/4 cups bread flour
- 1 teaspoon white sugar
- 1 1/2 teaspoons bread machine yeast

DIRECTIONS

1. Place ingredients into the pan of the bread machine in the order suggested by the manufacturer. Select the Dough cycle, and Start. (See Editor's Note for stand mixer instructions.)
2. Dough will be quite sticky and wet once cycle is completed; resist the temptation to add more flour. Place dough on a generously floured board, cover with a large bowl or greased plastic wrap, and let rest for 15 minutes.
3. Lightly flour baking sheets or line them with parchment paper. Using a serrated knife, divide dough into 2 pieces, and form each into a 3x14-inch oval. Place loaves on prepared sheets and dust lightly with flour. Cover, and let rise in a draft-free place for approximately 45 minutes.
4. Preheat oven to 425 degrees F (220 degrees C).
5. Spritz loaves with water. Place loaves in the oven, positioned on the middle rack. Bake until golden brown, 25 to 30 minutes.

TASTY BUNS

Servings: 12 | Prep: 20m | Cooks: 15m | Total: 1h20m

NUTRITION FACTS

Calories: 300 | Carbohydrates: 45.3g | Fat: 10.1g | Protein: 6.5g | Cholesterol: 2mg

INGREDIENTS

- 5 cups all-purpose flour
- 1/2 cup vegetable oil
- 2 (.25 ounce) packages dry yeast
- 1/4 cup white sugar
- 1 cup milk
- 1 teaspoon salt
- 3/4 cup water

DIRECTIONS

1. Stir together 2 cups flour and the yeast. In a separate bowl, heat milk, water, oil, sugar and salt to lukewarm in microwave. Add all at once to the flour mixture, and beat until smooth, about 3 minutes.
2. Mix in enough flour to make a soft dough, 2 to 3 cups. Mix well. Dust a flat surface with flour, turn dough out onto floured surface, and let rest under bowl for about 10 minutes.
3. Shape dough into 12 slightly flat balls, and place on greased baking sheet to rise until doubled in size.
4. Bake in a preheated 400 degrees F (200 degrees C) oven for 12 to 15 minutes.

MAYONNAISE BISCUITS

Servings: 12 | Prep: 10m | Cooks: 12m | Total: 22m

NUTRITION FACTS

Calories: 133 | Carbohydrates: 16.6g | Fat: 6.1g | Protein: 2.8g | Cholesterol: 4mg

INGREDIENTS

- 2 cups self-rising flour
- 6 tablespoons mayonnaise
- 1 cup milk

DIRECTIONS

1. Preheat oven to 400 degrees F (200 degrees C).
2. In a large bowl, stir together flour, milk, and mayonnaise until just blended. Drop by spoonfuls onto lightly greased baking sheets.
3. Bake for 12 minutes in the preheated oven, or until golden brown.

FRENCH BREAKFAST MUFFINS

Servings: 12 | Prep: 10m | Cooks: 25m | Total: 35m

NUTRITION FACTS

Calories: 207 | Carbohydrates: 25.2g | Fat: 11g | Protein: 2.6g | Cholesterol: 43mg

INGREDIENTS

- 1 1/2 cups all-purpose flour
- 1/2 cup milk
- 1/2 cup white sugar

- 1/3 cup butter, melted
- 1 1/2 teaspoons baking powder
- 1/4 cup white sugar
- 1/4 teaspoon ground nutmeg
- 1/2 teaspoon ground cinnamon
- 1/8 teaspoon salt
- 1/3 cup butter, melted
- 1 egg, lightly beaten

DIRECTIONS

1. Preheat oven to 350 degrees F (175 degrees C). Grease muffin cups or line with paper muffin liners.
2. In a medium mixing bowl, stir together flour, 1/2 cup sugar, baking powder, nutmeg and salt. Make a well in the center of the mixture. Stir together egg, milk and 1/3 cup melted butter. Add egg mixture to flour mixture; stir until just moistened (batter may be lumpy). Spoon batter into prepared muffin cups.
3. Bake in preheated oven for 20 to 25 minutes. Meanwhile, combine 1/4 cup sugar, cinnamon When muffins are finished baking, dip tops of muffins in the melted butter, and then in the cinnamon sugar mixture. Serve warm.

MIMI'S GIANT WHOLE-WHEAT BANANA-STRAWBERRY MUFFINS

Servings: 12 | Prep: 15m | Cooks: 20m | Total: 35m

NUTRITION FACTS

Calories: 212 | Carbohydrates: 38.1g | Fat: 5.9g | Protein: 4.2g | Cholesterol: 31mg

INGREDIENTS

- 2 eggs
- 3 bananas, mashed
- 1/2 cup unsweetened applesauce
- 2 cups whole wheat flour
- 1/4 cup vegetable oil
- 1 teaspoon baking soda
- 3/4 cup packed brown sugar
- 1 tablespoon ground cinnamon
- 1 teaspoon vanilla extract
- 1 cup frozen sliced strawberries

DIRECTIONS

1. Preheat the oven to 375 degrees F (190 degrees C). Grease 12 large muffin cups, or line with paper liners.
2. In a large bowl, whisk together the eggs, applesauce, oil, brown sugar, vanilla and bananas. Combine the flour, baking soda and cinnamon; Stir into the banana mixture until moistened. Stir in the strawberries until evenly distributed. Spoon batter into muffin cups until completely filled.
3. Bake for 20 minutes in the preheated oven, or until the tops of the muffins spring back when pressed lightly. Cool before removing from the muffin tins.

BANANA PUMPKIN BREAD

Servings: 12 | Prep: 20m | Cooks: 45m | Total: 1h5m

NUTRITION FACTS

Calories: 328 | Carbohydrates: 55.9g | Fat: 10.7g | Protein: 5.4g | Cholesterol: 31mg

INGREDIENTS

- 2 ripe bananas, mashed
- 1 teaspoon baking powder
- 2 eggs
- 1 teaspoon baking soda
- 1/3 cup vegetable oil
- 1/2 teaspoon salt
- 1 1/3 cups canned pumpkin puree
- 2 teaspoons pumpkin pie spice
- 1/2 cup honey
- 1 teaspoon ground cinnamon
- 1/2 cup white sugar
- 3/4 cup raisins (optional)
- 2 1/2 cups all-purpose flour
- 1/2 cup walnut pieces (optional)

DIRECTIONS

1. Preheat oven to 350 degrees F (175 degrees C). Grease an 9x5 inch loaf pan.
2. In a large bowl, stir together the mashed banana, eggs, oil, pumpkin, honey and sugar. Combine the flour, baking powder, baking soda, salt, pie spice and cinnamon, stir into the banana mixture until just combined. Fold in the raisins and walnuts if desired. Pour batter into the prepared pan.

3. Bake at 350 degrees F (175 degrees C) for 45 minutes, or until a toothpick inserted into the center of the loaf comes out clean. Cool loaf in the pan for 10 minutes before moving to a wire rack to cool completely.

LIGHT WHEAT ROLLS

Servings: 24 | Prep: 30m | Cooks: 15m | Total: 3h5m | Additional: 2h20m

NUTRITION FACTS

Calories: 140 | Carbohydrates: 22.5g | Fat: 4.4g | Protein: 3.4g | Cholesterol: 18mg

INGREDIENTS

- 2 (.25 ounce) packages active dry yeast
- 1 egg, beaten
- 1 3/4 cups warm water (110 degrees F/45 degrees C)
- 2 1/4 cups whole wheat flour
- 1/2 cup white sugar
- 2 1/2 cups all-purpose flour
- 1 teaspoon salt
- 1/4 cup butter, melted
- 1/4 cup butter, melted and cooled

DIRECTIONS

1. In a large bowl, dissolve yeast in warm water. Let stand until creamy, about 10 minutes.
2. Mix sugar, salt, 1/4 cup melted butter, egg, and whole wheat flour into yeast mixture. Stir in all-purpose flour, 1/2 cup at a time, until dough pulls away from the sides of the bowl. Turn dough out onto a well floured surface, and knead until smooth and elastic, about 8 minutes. Lightly oil a large bowl, place dough in bowl, and turn to coat. Cover with a damp cloth, and let rise in a warm place until doubled in volume, about 1 hour.
3. Punch down dough, cover, and let rise in warm place until doubled again, about 30 minutes.
4. Grease 2 dozen muffin cups. Punch down dough, and divide into two equal portions. Roll each into a 6x14 inch rectangle, and cut rectangle into twelve 7x1 inch strips. Roll strips up into spirals, and place into muffin cups. Brush tops with melted butter. Let rise uncovered in a warm place 40 minutes, or until doubled in bulk.
5. Preheat oven to 400 degrees F (200 degrees C). Bake for 12 to 15 minutes, or until golden brown. Remove from oven, and brush again with melted butter.

HONEY WHOLE WHEAT BREAD

Servings: 10 | Prep: 5m | Cooks: 3h | Total: 3h5m

NUTRITION FACTS

Calories: 180 | Carbohydrates: 33.4g | Fat: 3.5g | Protein: 5.2g | Cholesterol: 0mg

INGREDIENTS

- 1 1/8 cups warm water (110 degrees F/45 degrees C)
- 1 1/2 cups bread flour
- 3 tablespoons honey
- 2 tablespoons vegetable oil
- 1/3 teaspoon salt
- 1 1/2 teaspoons active dry yeast
- 1 1/2 cups whole wheat flour

DIRECTIONS

1. Add ingredients according to the manufacturer's directions to your bread machine. Use the wheat bread cycle and light color setting.

FUNNEL CAKES

Servings: 12 | Prep: 10m | Cooks: 10m | Total: 20m

NUTRITION FACTS

Calories: 263 | Carbohydrates: 36.8g | Fat: 9.8g | Protein: 6.9g | Cholesterol: 50mg

INGREDIENTS

- 1/2 teaspoon salt
- 1/4 cup white sugar
- 2 teaspoons baking powder
- 2 cups milk
- 3 2/3 cups all-purpose flour
- 1 quart vegetable oil for frying, or as needed
- 3 eggs
- 2 tablespoons confectioners' sugar, or as needed

DIRECTIONS

1. Mix salt, baking powder, and half the flour in a bowl. Set aside.
2. Cream eggs, sugar, and milk in a large bowl. Add flour mixture and beat until smooth. Continue to add remaining flour, but use only enough to achieve desired consistency. Batter will be thin enough to run through a funnel.
3. Heat the oil to 375 degrees F (190 degrees C) in an 8-inch skillet.
4. Put your finger over the bottom opening of the funnel, and fill the funnel with a generous 1/2 cup of the batter. Hold the funnel close to the surface of the oil, and release the batter into the oil while making a circular motion. Fry until golden brown. Use tongs and wide spatula to turn the cake over carefully. Fry the second side one minute. Drain on paper towels, and sprinkle with sifted confectioners' sugar.

APPLE BREAKFAST BREAD

Servings: 10 | Prep: 15m | Cooks: 1h | Total: 1h30m | Additional: 15m

NUTRITION FACTS

Calories: 279 | Carbohydrates: 43.2g | Fat: 10.5g | Protein: 4g | Cholesterol: 62mg

INGREDIENTS

- 1/2 cup butter
- 1 1/2 teaspoon salt
- 1 cup sugar
- 1 teaspoon ground cinnamon
- 2 eggs
- 1/2 teaspoon ground cloves
- 2 cups all-purpose flour
- 2 apples - peeled, cored and chopped
- 1 teaspoon baking soda

DIRECTIONS

1. Preheat oven to 350 degrees F (175 degrees C). Lightly grease an 8x4 inch loaf pan.
2. In a bowl, mix the butter and sugar until smooth and creamy. Beat in the eggs.
3. In a separate bowl, sift together the flour, baking soda, salt, cinnamon, and cloves. Mix into the butter mixture until moistened. Fold in the apples. Transfer to the prepared loaf pan.
4. Bake 1 hour in the preheated oven, until a toothpick inserted in the center comes out clean. Cool in the pan for 15 minutes before removing to a wire rack to cool completely.

GARLIC CHEESE BISCUITS

Servings: 10 | Prep: 10m | Cooks: 10m | Total: 20m

NUTRITION FACTS

Calories: 152 | Carbohydrates: 18.3g | Fat: 7.1g | Protein: 4.1g | Cholesterol: 19mg

INGREDIENTS

- 2 cups buttermilk baking mix
- 1/4 cup butter, melted
- 2/3 cup milk
- 1/2 teaspoon garlic powder
- 1/2 cup shredded Cheddar cheese

DIRECTIONS

1. Preheat oven to 450 degrees F (230 degrees C).
2. Combine baking mix, milk and cheddar cheese in mixing bowl. Beat with wooden spoon till soft dough forms.
3. Drop dough by spoonfuls onto ungreased cookie sheet. Bake 8-10 minutes until golden brown.
4. Mix butter and garlic powder and brush over warm biscuits before removing from cookie sheet.

EASY OATMEAL MUFFINS

Servings: 12 | Prep: 15m | Cooks: 25m | Total: 40m

NUTRITION FACTS

Calories: 136 | Carbohydrates: 17.8g | Fat: 5.9g | Protein: 3.2g | Cholesterol: 17mg

INGREDIENTS

- 1 cup milk
- 1 cup all-purpose flour
- 1 cup quick cooking oats
- 1/4 cup white sugar
- 1 egg
- 2 teaspoons baking powder
- 1/4 cup vegetable oil
- 1/2 teaspoon salt

DIRECTIONS

1. Preheat oven to 425 degrees F (220 degrees C). Grease muffin cups or line with paper muffin liners.
2. In a small bowl, combine milk and oats; let soak for 15 minutes.
3. In a separate bowl, beat together egg and oil; stir in oatmeal mixture. In a third bowl, sift together flour, sugar, baking powder and salt. Stir flour mixture into wet ingredients, just until combined. Spoon batter into prepared muffin cups until cups are 2/3 full.
4. Bake in preheated oven for 20 to 25 minutes, until a toothpick inserted into the center of a muffin comes out clean.

EASY OATMEAL MUFFINS

Servings: 24 | Prep: 20m | Cooks: 15m | Total: 35m

NUTRITION FACTS

Calories: 118 | Carbohydrates: 17.4g | Fat: 4.9g | Protein: 1.6g | Cholesterol: 16mg

INGREDIENTS

- 1 quart vegetable oil for deep-frying
- 2/3 cup milk
- 1 1/2 cups all-purpose flour
- 2 eggs, beaten
- 1 tablespoon white sugar
- 1 tablespoon vegetable oil
- 2 teaspoons baking powder
- 3 cups apples - peeled, cored and chopped
- 1/2 teaspoon salt
- 1 cup cinnamon sugar

DIRECTIONS

1. Heat the oil in a deep-fryer or electric skillet to 375 degrees F (190 degrees C).
2. In a large bowl, stir together the flour, sugar, baking powder and salt. Pour in the milk, eggs and oil and stir until well blended. Mix in apples until they are evenly distributed.
3. Drop spoonfuls of the batter into the hot oil and fry until golden on both sides, about 5 minutes depending on the size. Fry in smaller batches so they are not crowded. Remove from the hot oil using a slotted spoon and drain briefly on paper towels. Toss with cinnamon sugar while still warm.

MINI PUMPKIN BUTTERSCOTCH MUFFINS

Servings: 48 | Prep: 15m | Cooks: 10m | Total: 25m

NUTRITION FACTS

Calories: 75 | Carbohydrates: 10.5g | Fat: 3.2g | Protein: 0.8g | Cholesterol: 13mg

INGREDIENTS

- 1 3/4 cups all-purpose flour
- 1/4 teaspoon baking powder
- 1/2 cup brown sugar
- 1/2 teaspoon salt
- 1/2 cup white sugar
- 2 eggs
- 1 teaspoon ground cinnamon
- 1/2 cup melted butter
- 1/2 teaspoon ground ginger
- 1 cup canned pumpkin
- 1/2 teaspoon ground nutmeg
- 1 (6 ounce) package butterscotch chips
- 1 teaspoon baking soda

DIRECTIONS

1. Preheat oven to 350 degrees F (175 degrees C). Grease mini-muffin pan with cooking spray.
2. Sift together the flour, brown sugar, white sugar, cinnamon, ginger, nutmeg, baking soda, baking powder, and salt into a large bowl. Whisk together the eggs, butter, and pumpkin in a separate bowl. Mix the flour mixture with the egg mixture. Stir in the butterscotch chips; pour into each cup of the muffin pan to about 3/4 full.
3. Bake in preheated oven until a toothpick inserted into the center of a muffin comes out clean, 10 to 12 minutes.

QUICK AND EASY YORKSHIRE PUDDING

Servings: 12 | Prep: 10m | Cooks: 30m | Total: 40m

NUTRITION FACTS

Calories: 83 | Carbohydrates: 9g | Fat: 3.7g | Protein: 3.3g | Cholesterol: 53mg

INGREDIENTS

- 3 eggs
- 1 cup milk

- 1 cup all-purpose flour
- 2 tablespoons butter

DIRECTIONS

1. Preheat oven to 375 degrees F (190 degrees C).
2. in a medium bowl, beat eggs with milk. Stir in flour. Set aside.
3. Divide butter evenly into the twelve cups of a muffin tin, about 1/2 teaspoon per cup. Place tin in oven to melt butter, 2 to 5 minutes. Remove tin from oven, and distribute batter evenly among buttery cups.
4. Bake in preheated oven 5 minutes. Reduce heat to 350 degrees F (175 degrees C), and bake 25 minutes more or until puffed and golden.

BROWN SUGAR BANANA NUT BREAD

Servings: 12 | Prep: 15m | Cooks: 1h | Total: 1h15m

NUTRITION FACTS

Calories: 273 | Carbohydrates: 37.9g | Fat: 12.1g | Protein: 4.5g | Cholesterol: 51mg

INGREDIENTS

- 1/2 cup butter, softened
- 2 cups all-purpose flour
- 1 cup brown sugar
- 3 teaspoons baking powder
- 2 eggs
- 1/2 teaspoon salt
- 1 tablespoon vanilla extract
- 1/2 cup chopped walnuts
- 4 very ripe bananas, mashed

DIRECTIONS

1. Preheat oven to 350 degrees F (175 degrees C). Lightly grease a 9x5 inch loaf pan.
2. In a large bowl, cream together the butter and sugar until light and fluffy. Stir in the eggs one at a time, beating well with each addition. Stir in vanilla and banana. In a separate bowl, sift together flour, baking powder, and salt.

3. Blend the banana mixture into the flour mixture; stir just to combine. Fold in walnuts. Pour batter into prepared pan.
4. Bake in preheated oven for 1 hour, until a toothpick inserted into center of loaf comes out clean.

LOWER FAT BANANA BREAD

Servings: 12 | Prep: 15m | Cooks: 1h | Total: 1h15m

NUTRITION FACTS

Calories: 169 | Carbohydrates: 28.8g | Fat: 4.9g | Protein: 3.1g | Cholesterol: 31mg

INGREDIENTS

- 2/3 cup white sugar
- 1 2/3 cups all-purpose flour
- 1/4 cup margarine, softened
- 1 teaspoon baking soda
- 2 eggs
- 1/2 teaspoon salt
- 1 cup mashed bananas
- 1/4 teaspoon baking powder
- 1/4 cup water

DIRECTIONS

1. Preheat oven to 350 degrees F (175 degrees C). Spray one 9x5x3 inch loaf pan with a non-stick cooking spray.
2. In a medium bowl, beat the white sugar and margarine or butter until smooth and creamy. Beat in the eggs, water and bananas with the sugar mixture until it is well blended.
3. Mix in the flour, baking soda, salt and baking powder just until the mixture is moistened. Be sure to scrape the sides of the bowl to blend all ingredients.
4. Bake at 350 degrees F (175 degree C) for about 60 minutes. Bread is done when the top is firm to the touch and a golden brown color. Time will vary according to loaf size and oven type. When bread is removed from oven, allow it to cool on it's side for 10 minutes, then remove from pan and let cool on a rack. This bread is also excellent if you add mini chocolate chips or small fruit pieces to the mix just before baking.

PLAIN CAKE DOUGHNUTS

Servings: 12 | Prep: 10m | Cooks: 15m | Total: 25m

NUTRITION FACTS

Calories: 202 | Carbohydrates: 25g | Fat: 10.1g | Protein: 3g | Cholesterol: 21mg

INGREDIENTS

- 2 cups all-purpose flour
- 1 dash ground nutmeg
- 1/2 cup white sugar
- 2 tablespoons melted butter
- 1 teaspoon salt
- 1/2 cup milk
- 1 tablespoon baking powder
- 1 egg, beaten
- 1 1/4 teaspoon ground cinnamon
- 1 quart oil for frying

DIRECTIONS

1. Heat oil in deep-fryer to 375 degrees F (190 degrees C).
2. In a large bowl, sift together flour, sugar, salt, baking powder, cinnamon and nutmeg. Mix in butter until crumbly. Stir in milk and egg until smooth. Knead lightly, then turn out onto a lightly floured surface. Roll or pat to 1/4 inch thickness. Cut with a doughnut cutter, or use two round biscuit cutters of different sizes.
3. Carefully drop doughnuts into hot oil, a few at a time. Do not overcrowd pan or oil may overflow. Fry, turning once, for 3 minutes or until golden. Drain on paper towels.